The Spirit

of Sport

Essays About Sport And Values

Edited by

John W. Molloy, Jr.
Richard C. Adams

Wyndham Hall Press

THE SPIRIT OF SPORT

Essays About Sport and Values

edited by

John W. Molloy, Jr.
Richard C. Adams

Library of Congress Catalog Card Number
87-050692

ISBN 1-55605-012-7

The editors
dedicate their efforts in this book
to their respective parents,

John W. and Betty Grant Molloy
Ralph E. and Myrtle Taylor Adams

TABLE OF CONTENTS

i

ACKNOWLEDGMENTS

The editors wish to acknowledge their gratitude to:

Mr. Richard W. Conklin and the Public Relations Department of the University of Notre Dame for permission to use the photographs of:

The Dome of the Administration Building*
The Memorial Library §
The Stadium*

and to quote the chorus of the Notre Dame Victory March.

*photographs courtesy of Richard C. Adams
§photograph courtesy of the Sports Information Department, University of Notre Dame

Jacques Cyr, Coordinator of Media Production Services of the University of Ottawa, for his assistance in providing the photograph titled "Racquetball Doubles,"* and the permission to use it, and to the following persons who assisted in making the photograph possible, along with their permission to use it, Gunther Ottlewski, Jack Goldfield, Leonard Farber, and Saul Ross.

*photograph courtesy of Media Production Services, the University of Ottawa.

Nate Greenberg and the Boston Bruins Public Relations Department for background material and for permission to use the photograph of Michael O'Connell.

Rosemary Hall of Quinnipiac College for secretarial assistance in preparing the manuscript.

The Embassy of Ireland, Ottawa, Ontario, Canada for assistance in providing prints of the following photographs along with the permission to use them from their owners, to whom we also express our gratitude:

The Irish Independent for the photograph titled "Hurling: A game of skill, courage, and speed."
The Irish Press for the photograph titled "Catching a High Ball: A feature of Gaelic football."

Dr. Leonard J. Kent of Quinnipiac College for his assistance with a critical reading of the manuscript.

The Rev. Edward C. Krause for his interest in, and assistance with, the preparation of the manuscript.

Dave Neubert and the Seattle Seahawks Public Relations Department for permission to use the photograph of Joe Nash.

Robert A. Parcella for permission to use the photograph titled "Olympic Arch."

Teri Pettinato of Guilford, Connecticut for her interest in the project and for permission to use the photograph titled "At the Ball Game."

Michael and Joyce Psaros for permission to use the photograph of their son, Michael George Psaros, titled "At the Ball Game," and the photograph of their family titled "Family Skating."

iii

LIST OF ILLUSTRATIONS

*Courtesy of Richard C. Adams

LIST OF PHOTOGRAPHS

PREFACE

by John W. Molloy, Jr.

Sport is an important area in most people's lives. As such, it reflects many of the dimensions of our personal and social lives and we can see something of our greatness in it. Sport also means fun and games. As such, it appeals to the child in all of us. Clearly, sport creates many different values.

The purpose of this book is to present a work which will be useful to persons interested in sport and the values associated with it. Accordingly, the editors have invited people to discuss sport and value from the different perspectives of their own interest and involvement in it. We have asked them to share their experience and their understanding. The book is meant to be a sampling of such views rather than a complete survey of the many possibilities.

In presenting this collection of essays, we are not attempting to define sport, although most of the articles are concerned with experience in competitive sports of various kinds. Value is not defined but relates in a general way to various kinds of fulfillment realized in relation to sport. There is no ideological thrust in the book. However, we have been concerned to elicit discussion about the best of sport and its related values. Even so, we recognize the pros and cons of various kinds of sports experience.

It is our hope that this collection of essays will, like the sporting experience itself at its best, contribute to the kind of understanding which helps us all to become fulfilled as better human beings.

Quincy, Massachusetts

THE SPIRIT OF SPORT: AN INTRODUCTION

by Richard C. Adams

We can think of the "spirit of sport" as something which is felt and immediate--a shared emotion and enthusiasm. We can also think of it as a basic framework of ideas or a perspective of understanding which is held in relation to sport. Clearly these are related meanings. Our feelings go along with our thinking. Both of these possible meanings of the spirit of sport would, I think, be appropriate to this book. At the same time, the editors do not have a special definition of the phrase in mind in using it as the primary title. Our contributors have related to it with complete freedom. In doing so they, of course, best speak for themselves. It is not my intention to infringe upon this freedom in any way in the remarks that follow.

In this introduction I present something of my own thinking on some of the issues which the essays that follow will often address in greater detail. I will also refer to writings which I have found helpful, and for which I am especially grateful, without attempting to give a complete listing of the references which might be relevant to the issues involved: the spirit of play, the spirit of excellence, the spirit of freedom, and the religious spirit.

The Spirit of Play

....it's the last of the ninth, the score is 3-2, the count is 3-2, with two away -- there's the wind up...

"Sport," a friend of mine once remarked, "is fun just because it is so serious." My friend was right. It is serious. It is serious because it matters what happens. And then again, it is fun, because, in a sense, it really doesn't matter after all. Anyone who watched or took part in the 1986 Baseball World Series in any way experienced sport at its most serious peak. The

1

kind of intensity portrayed in the fictional moment above was felt more than once by everybody on both sides. Elation alternated with anguish in rapid succession. Eventually, of course, these became the primary moods of the winners and losers respectively. The New York Mets' locker room overflowed with joy, while that of the Boston Red Sox seemed to be filled with disappointment. In New York, the Mets fans went all out in their applause and in their happiness at being No. 1.

The Red Sox also returned to their fans' acclaim, and their welcome home was no less enthusiastic. Nor was it any less honorable. There was neither need for, nor show of, despair. The Red Sox had played well, and they would go on to another year and to other games--more determined than ever to show both rivals and fans their effort and their ability. And their fans would rekindle the flames of their hopes.

One of the reasons why sport can be both fun and serious is that its victories and defeats are not final. What is lost today may well be won back tomorrow. The "final" score is final only for today's event and not for those which will be played in the future. But there are other reasons, too. For one thing, a sporting event can be a means to an end beyond itself, such as a career, and at the same time be an end in itself--where the "play is the thing." So far as the first of these is concerned, performance in the game and the game's outcome can be quite serious. Reputations, jobs, and money can all be on the line. The social context in which sport takes place is a highly competitive one. The stakes are high and the consequences of wins and losses are more telling, with the losses less easily recovered. At the same time, as Michael Novak points out, sport partakes of the "kingdom of ends." Like art, love, and worship, it is complete in each moment of the action's unfolding. The performance and the "win" are their own reward (8). There is, of course, a certain tension between these aspects. This tension often leads to the dispute as to whether the playful or the serious are the most important in sport. But perhaps it is not an either/or situation. They are equally important, as are winning and performance.

Johan Huizinga, in discussing the serious and non-serious aspects of play, relates his thought to that of Plato. In the book **Homo**

2

Ludens, Huizinga writes: "The true poet, says Socrates in Plato's **Symposium,** must be tragic and comic at once, and the whole of human life must be felt as a blend of tragedy and comedy" (6: p. 145). Thus Huizinga calls attention to Plato's understanding of the serious and not serious character of life itself, of which sport is, after all, a part.

The ancient Greeks had a word for play (spoudegeloios) which combined the ideas of its serious and non-serious aspects. Over the centuries the idea changed so that the idea of play became opposite in meaning to that of the serious, or subordinate to it. Perhaps we need to recover the idea of play in the ancient Greek sense in our understanding of both sport and life.[1]

To see to it that both sport and life combine the best of the seriousness of competition and the delight of play is a social task. It also presents a task for philosophical understanding.

Saul Ross addresses the philosophical task in relation to sport. He speaks to it from out of his own experience in racquetball--a sport in which many persons participate. In doing so he argues convincingly that sport can be both contest and play, and that each of these aspects can be a source of joy to the participants.

The Spirit of Excellence

   Roger Bannister...Althea Gibson...Jim Thorpe...Virginia
   Wade...Jim Craig...Diego Maradona...Martina Navratilova

The names of those who have exhibited athletic excellence call up our admiration. People involved in sport look for many things. For some, it is the event itself which counts--the performance--the demonstration of athletic ability and excellence. For others, the winning itself, or the fringe benefits, of whatever kind, are as important, or more so. But whatever our interests and motivations, athletic beauty, skill, and strength, when demonstrated, command our attention. The heroes of ancient Greece were "god-like"--or were thought actually to be the offspring of the gods, as was Hercules, one of the patron gods of strength and the athletic event. Today our heroes are the "charismatic" persons who capture our imagination and our praise with their superior talents--whatever these may be. We are automatically drawn to them.

Sport, as we are reminded by Robert J. Higgs, is the natural arena for the heroic. Every walk of life has its heroes, but in sport the doing of mighty deeds in the face of the odds is especially visible. We gravitate to these deeds and to their doers because they hold up something to which we also aspire. They inspire in us a sense of our own potential as human beings. They bring to us a measure of participation in its achievement. The hero or heroine are such because they relate us to something more than ourselves. Their struggles and their victories take us out of and beyond the limits of our ordinary lives with their undramatic gains and losses. We stand with the heroes whom we admire. Our lives are heightened by them (5: pp. 137-158).

Quality means not only excellence, it also means the "best." When we think of these attributes as applied to athletes, we necessarily think of the professional athletes in our culture (the "Pro's"). They represent an achievement at the peak of athletic attainment and they quite rightly receive our attention. And from those whom we respect the most, we also demand the most. Thus the professionals often come under considerable critical fire. What they exhibit to us has been refined in a thousand ways. The Greek word <u>heros</u> meant the embodiment of composite ideals of mind and body. To this we still aspire, and we therefore ask for much from those who excel. To reach professional status, and to stay there without becoming involved in the problems which plague the sport world today, demands a sound mind and a sound body indeed (5: p. 143).

The same thing is, of course, needed of heroes everywhere--the scientist, the peacemaker--one could think of many kinds of excellence to which people dedicate themselves. But the thing that marks the athletic hero is the public nature and the objectivity of the deeds as they are being done. They are there for millions to see--for <u>all</u> to see. Witness the victory of the U.S.A. hockey team at the 1980 Olympics! Witness Superbowl XXI!

In our own day it is the media in all of its forms which most makes us witness to the achievement of athletic excellence.

Not only does the media bear witness to excellence, it also keeps the records of it for us, reminding us of its lasting values. Moreover, there is also the story involved in any achievement, the story of the personal struggle, the important and often hard decisions which are behind the objective attainment. It is this which finally adds the fully human dimension to our appreciation of it.

It is to the telling of the story, along with its witness to professional excellence, that my colleague, John W. Molloy, Jr., turns his attention in sharing with us the stories of two professional athletes, Joe Nash of the Seattle Seahawks, and Michael O'Connell of the Detroit Red Wings. Both of these men have travelled the often-difficult road to professional status in sport. In doing so, each has given to us something of greatness in themselves and in sport to admire.

Perhaps, in some respects, no figure better epitomizes the athletic hero of ancient Greece than the image which we have of the winner of the Olympic contests. Standing in the temple of Zeus at the end of the festivities and games, the hero was awarded a simple wreath of wild olive leaves--the crowning recognition of achievement. Of such an image E. Norman Gardiner writes:

> ...whatever its origin this custom of rewarding the victor with no other prize than a wreath of leaves set an example of athletic purity--Indeed, the Olympic crown is a lesson in sportsmanship for all time, reminding us that the true sportsman contends not for the value of the prize but for the honour of victory and not for his own honour only but for that of his country, his state, his school, his side (3: p. 36).

We know, of course, that the ideal of this model of purity existed only sporadically and imperfectly in the games of ancient Greece, as it does today; yet it serves, as does any ideal, to bring to us a vision of another dimension of what we might be at our best (10).

The Olympic motto "Higher, Faster, Stronger," aptly sums up that stretching of the self which is essential to athletic achievement. Such an ideal spurs on those who do achieve, and spurs us on in our admiration for them. Those who continue to push to new records are truly deserving of our praise. Reaching the seemingly impossible, as Roger Bannister did when he ran the four minute mile in 1954, thrills us all with its accomplishment. But surely our thrill is not with the new mark alone. It is also with the all-out effort involved in making it. In fact, the attempt itself, the giving of one's best, is perhaps what moves the deeper part of our praise. What we most admire, in Grantland Rice's phrase is "the uphill heart" (5: p. 221). This counts most in our recognition of those who achieve the highest, the fastest, and the strongest.

But equally we can appreciate it in those who, perhaps less fortunate than others in their natural gifts, nevertheless give their all in the struggle to attain perfection. It is of these that Michele Gelfman writes, sharing with us her experiences with the Special Olympics and with those "quiet heroes" who, bringing to us an exhibition of sport in its purity, are deserving of our highest praise.

Sometime around the sixth century B.C.E., the Chinese scholar and philosopher whom we commonly know as Confucius, made the observation that when things go well in the family they also go well in the village. Such well being then reaches from the village to influence the district and, ultimately, the nation and the world.

It is a commonplace of psychology that the springboard of our developing personality, and of our fundamental sense of trust and worth, comes from the early years of our childhood. As Confucius wisely saw, our sense of values and the desire for excellence of any kind begin with the family. Truly, heroes are made as well as born. The nurture which we give or receive in our initial family situation is all-important to eventual success.

Linda Morgan and Albert K. Wimmer have both been very much involved in the parental task of nurturing in families that are active in sports. In their joint article they share with us the memories and day-by-day encounters which this has involved. Sharing and individual encouragement, intimacy and distancing, are all a part of the sport-oriented family game.

The Spirit of Freedom

It was at 4:15 p.m. on February 4, 1987, that Dennis Conner and his crew brought the yacht Stars and Stripes of the U.S.A. to a 1-minute-59-second lead victory that completed a 4-0 sweep over the yacht Kookaburra III of Australia.

The America's Cup competition was many things. It was a contest between sailing crews and their skippers which called for the best of yachting skills. It was also, in a sense, a contest of technologies--of design--and of engineering. It became a focus, for a brief time, of the friendly rivalry in the sport of yacht racing between two nations, carrying with it the loyalty and pride of their peoples. It was also a challenge to the exercise of responsible freedom.

Sporting events require self assertion and competition. They also require freedom and cooperation. As Lynne Belaief notes:

....Assertiveness, alone or with a team, is requisite to develop the very content of a game within its given form. One cannot remain powerless, passive, and non-creative and also be participating in the sport. This is the demand that freedom be expressed (freedom perceived as self determination within a set of rules we agree to obey). Moreover, freedom exists in the more fundamental level that we made it all up. We can change the form if desired, and we can void any results that betray the rules, call it a foul and do it again... (2: p. 55).

As Lynne Belaief perceives, it is the balance of self interest and common interest that makes freedom in terms of sporting competition possible. We cooperate to compete, and the rules prescribe the character of the contest, setting limits to the conflict involved and protecting the safety of the participants.

But, of course, the rules can be violated and injuries can come about which are deliberately inflicted rather than being accidentally incurred. Such a resort to violence simply to win an event, however, misses out on a more important victory. This

7

is the achievement by both parties of the experience of responsible freedom exercised in play.

Thinking of freedom in sport in this way, the main question is not just who dominates in the sport contest, but whether we shall stand or fall together. Victory in sport, in the fullest sense, includes the establishment of mutual trust and respect.

The scientist and theologian Pierre Teilhard de Chardin gives excellent expression to this idea in his book **Building the Earth** (11: pp. 26-32). Assessing the vision and hope of democracy for the building of man's future, he points out the needed "Personalism" which it represents, along with its "Universalism." Personalism refers to the unique potential and rights of each individual. Universalism ensures and protects these for all. Both of these are important if we are to achieve that which in Teilhard's words "Everyone wants," "something larger, finer, better for mankind" (11: p. 33).

The articles by Sean Egan and Frans De Wachter are relevant to this concern. In his article, Sean Egan discusses the spirit of "the fighting Irish." The spirit of the Celts, as he describes it, is one which is dedicated to the achievement of self identity. It loves freedom and democracy and is proud of its country and ethnic heritage. It is a "never-give-up" spirit in its commitment to the attainment of these values.

There is a saying that "Everyone is Irish on St. Patrick's Day." In Sean Egan's discussion of the contributions of the Celts to sport, and of their commitment to the values of self-identity and freedom, we can find ample reason why one might well feel this way.

Frans De Wachter addresses the possible contribution of sport, and more especially of sport education, to the concern for peace at the international level. He assesses the relation of sport to militarism, aggression, the demolishing of enemy images, and to the development of conflict solving competence. In the last of these, in the parallels which sport has with democracy, he finds a significant hope. And in the sporting experience he finds, too, the intimation of a deeper victory.

The Religious Spirit

In the summer of 1972, I attended a gathering of people interested in the dialogue between the religions of the world. Spiritual leaders from all of the various religions were present for us to hear. I wish to recall an incident with one of them. He was asked about the meaning of religion. He smiled as he turned to a person nearby, who then placed himself on the floor. The speaker immediately reached down and gave the assistant his hand, helping him to his feet. "There," he said (or words to this effect), "that is religion."[2]

The gesture which was demonstrated in this incident is not, of course, sufficient to our understanding of the whole of religion. Yet few would deny that it does represent something which is basic in all religious expression--to be genuinely concerned with the well-being of others.

Can this concern be carried into the sport arena? I suggest that it can be, and that we indeed see it demonstrated there all the time. Anyone who has participated in sport in any way knows of countless ordinary examples of the gesture described above. One player often assists another in a similar way--not only on his or her own team, but sometimes on the opposing team as well. We have all seen it. It might even be after the put out of a slide into second base. However slight or unnoticed, these actions suggest the assertion of the attitude of "good will" toward another. In the exchange of genuine handshakes after a spirited contest we have a more prominent example of the same thing.

Such actions point us to the deeper heart of the question of goodness in sport. We are what we are as a whole person wherever we go--onto the playing field or into the stands.[3] The extent of our concern for others involves a fundamental choice however it is expressed. To have sport at its best, we must surely have some kind of moral vision. Along with the "never-give-up" attitude so essential to achievement in sport, there is perhaps also the need for the vision of something which is worthy of our giving up all.[4]

The spirit of sport as presented so far in this article, and as discussed by various authors in the book, is a composite one--it holds up an ideal of many dimensions. Perhaps no more fitting symbol of such a composite ideal could be found than in that suggested by the name of "Notre Dame." Founded in 1842 by Father Edward Sorin, C.S.C., the University of Notre Dame has become associated in the minds of many with both athletic and academic excellence. As discussed by Edward W. "Moose" Krause, the spirit of Notre Dame means many things. It means a winning spirit, it means a fighting spirit, it means a spirit of excellence. But above all, it means a deeply religious spirit. In sharing his experience of these with us, "Moose" Krause touches us at the heart with those things which are of the best in sport, and in life.

In summary, sport appeals to us and has value for us because it is an area where many of the value issues in our lives are experienced in a focused kind of way. Sport reflects and shapes our values.

The interplay of fun and seriousness, of work and play, and of the tragic and comic aspects of our existence is involved in sport. To experience sport and to reflect upon it can be of help to us in understanding this interplay--for the sake of our living more fulfilled lives.

The desire for fulfillment, and the struggle to achieve it, becomes focused in sport in terms of the excellence of athletic performance. Sport is physical. It embodies the struggle for excellence in a highly visible way. As it does so, it becomes the practical testing ground for a whole range of values which make for excellence in the fullest sense: truth, beauty, goodness, freedom, justice, equality. The performance in sport, along with the wins and losses, becomes the occasion for discovering, creating, and measuring these values in a down-to-earth and concrete way.

This encounter in sport with values and with value choices is both individual and social in character. The cooperative competition required for sport is a forthright assertion of both the "I am" and the "We are" aspects of our living. As such, sport provides a widely available opportunity for the learning and the exercise of responsible freedom. In competitive sport at its best, this opportunity is used to achieve the winning

10

of mutual trust and respect on the part of all those involved in the contest. This victory includes, but also supercedes, the value of winning in the usual sense.

Hence, sport leads us to the basic questions of our moral choice. At this point it challenges us to courageous commitment to a fundamental allegiance. The exact statement of this allegiance, quite rightly, takes different forms. In thinking of it and in closing my remarks in this essay, I quote the following lines from the Portuguese poet, Fernando da Sena:

To be great, be complete
Nothing yours exaggerate or exclude
Be all yourself in everything
So in the lake, the eternal moon shines
So high it lives.[5]

Hamden, Connecticut

11

NOTES

1. The word <u>spoudegeloios</u> combines the word for "serious" (<u>spoude</u>) with the word for "mirth provoking" (<u>geloios</u>). Play is grave and merry at the same time (7: p. 104).

David L. Miller points out, however, that Plato also regarded the "play" of life as secondary in the final analysis to a higher seriousness (7: p. 106). This brings up a further philosophical problem which he and others have addressed. See the discussion in Robert J. Higgs, <u>Sports: A Reference Guide</u> (5: pp. 210ff).

See the discussion of this also in Filmer S.C. Northrop's book <u>Man, Nature, and God</u>. New York: Simon and Schuster, 1962, pp. 100-112; 246-255.

2. This conference, titled "Word Out of Silence," is described in <u>Cross Currents</u>, Volume 24, 1974.

3. As noted by the character "Shivas Irons" in Michael Murphy's book <u>Golf in the Kingdom</u>. New York: Delta, 1972, p. 42. We reveal ourselves in a public way in sport. Also we both measure and are measured by that which we applaud and will pay for (5: pp. 159-167).

4. In speaking of this, Teilhard writes:

> The loadstone which must magnetize and purify the energies in us, whose growing surplus is presently dissipated in useless wars and perverse refinements, I would place in the last analysis, in the gradual manifestation of some essential object, whose total wealth, more precious than gold, more seductive than any beauty, would be for man grown adult, the Grail and the Eldorado in which the ancient conquerors believed; something tangible, for the possession of which it would be infinitely good to lay down one's life (11: pp. 36-37).

In the final analysis, the bottom line of our morality must incorporate the love of God.

5. Quoted by Filmer S.C. Northrop in his book <u>The Prolegomena to a 1985 Philosophiae Naturalis Principia Mathematica</u>. Woodbridge: Oxbow, 1985, p. 54.

BIBLIOGRAPHY

1. Bannister, Roger. The Four Minute Mile. New York: Dodd, Mead, & Co., 1955.

2. Belaief, Lynne. "Meanings of the Body." Journal of the Philosophy of Sport. Volume 9, 1977, pp. 50-67.

3. Gardiner, E. Norman. Athletics of the Ancient World. London: Oxford University Press, 1930.

4. Higgs, Robert J. Laurel and Thorn. Lexington: The University Press of Kentucky, 1981.

5._____. Sports: A Reference Guide. Westport: Greenwood Press, 1982.

6. Huizinga, Johan. Homo Ludens: A Study of the Play Element in Culture. Translated by R.F.C. Hull. Boston: Beacon Press, 1960.

7. Miller, David L. Gods and Games: Toward a Theology of Play. New York: World, 1970.

8. Novak, Michael. The Joy of Sports: End Zones, Bases, Baskets, Balls, and the Consecration of the American Spirit. New York: Basic Books, 1976.

9. Rahner, Hugo. Man at Play. New York: Herder and Herder, 1967.

10. Segrave, Jeffrey, and Chu, Donald. Olympism. Champaign, IL: Human Kinetics, 1981.

11. Teilhard de Chardin, Pierre. Building the Earth. Denville: Dimension Books, 1965.

EDUCATION FOR PEACE IN SPORTS EDUCATION

by Frans De Wachter

The International Charter of Physical Education and Sports approved at the 20th UNESCO General Conference in 1978 includes this sentence:

> Through cooperation and the pursuit of mutual interests in the universal language of physical education and sport, all peoples will contribute to the preservation of lasting peace, universal respect and friendship, and will thus create a propitious climate for solving international problems.

This statement indicates how this charter applies the general objective of UNESCO to the world of sport. The objective is to put education, science, and culture to the service of the promotion of the respect for human dignity and of better international understanding. This same concern can be perceived in the activities of the International Council For Sport and Physical Education (ICSPE), which is actually a suborganization of UNESCO. Let us not forget that Philip J. Noel-Baker, who was awarded the Nobel Prize for Peace in 1959, was president of the ICSPE for sixteen years. And under the auspices of the same organization, a major congress was organized in Helsinki in 1982 on "sport and international understanding." The specific intention was to apply the ideas of the Helsinki conference, of 1975, for security and cooperation in Europe to the world of sport. And in the Olympic movement, there is also a long tradition of glorifying sport as a contribution to peace; thus, in 1983, in Osaka, Japan, an international symposium was held on the Olympic movement and world peace.

However, sport is a very rich but also a varied activity. It can signify, reinforce, or create very different kinds of human interaction: blind robotization as well as play experience, coercive drive for profit as well as convivial bodily awareness, social antagonism as well as cooperation. Sports is too ambiguous an interaction process and does not simply promote, by

17

its naked presence, peaceful relationships, no more than every science serves social progress, all music improves character, or every religion unites people as brothers and sisters. It is my view that "the spirit of sport" may best be understood as a normative idea or an ethical task.

For this reason, the UNESCO text should not be read as a descriptive text in which an actual relationship between sport and peace is established. The text is more meaningful if it is read normatively and educationally. If sport is not automatically a factor for peace, it can only become such a factor on the basis of a conscious educational intervention. This makes use of certain potentials in sport to form attitudes that create a favorable climate in which something like peace can be established. This is, therefore, my point of departure. It is possible that athletic education offers a fruitful educational opportunity for education for peace. It is to this question that I want to restrict myself. To what extent is this possible? What are the positive elements that sport-education can use when we are interested in promoting peace attitudes in the educational process? What precisely are these attitudes? In order to answer these questions, I must first define with more precision the concepts of "peace" and "peace education."

Peace and peace education

The concept of peace can have two meanings. First, it could refer to a situation without conflicts, that is, a situation without private interests that must be defended. This is a situation where specific interests are no longer at stake or where the interests of each individual would coincide with the general interest. This is a utopian notion of peace, which is meaningful as long as it does not lose its theological roots. Typical of the Biblical concept of peace is that this condition is situated beyond history, in the heavenly paradise where the lion lies down with the lamb. But when the utopia loses this theological context and is considered an objective that must be achieved in human history, it will probably produce its very opposite: oppression and violence. For the negation of the opposition is the negation of individual differences. This would lead to the elimination of everyone who does not identify with one viewpoint. This suppression of the dissident is the way to a totalitarian vision of society.

Peace in its operational, non-utopian meaning is not defined as a condition without conflicts but as a situation where people are capable of rational, non-violent conflict resolution. One does not eliminate conflicts, but learns to live with them in a reasonable way. For reasonableness is non-violence. Reason permits problems and differences of opinion to be reasonably discussed and resolved instead of being assailed in the immediacy of physical or ideological violence. Non-violent conflict resolution is then the opting for a solution that does not consist of the elimination or suppression of the weaker party.

Our notion of peace education must also renounce premature utopian expectations. Here, too, a warning is appropriate against too-utopian haste. Peace education is not a direct peace factor. World peace must be achieved in the hard reality of international situations by politicians who conclude treaties and secure precarious balances of power. Education can only develop subjective attitudes in individuals. These attitudes include the readiness and the competence to resolve conflicts non-violently, without victimizing the weak. Now such an attitude is not a sufficient condition for peace. Wars, for example, are caused by very complex social mechanisms without individuals needing them or nourishing mutual hate.

Nevertheless, such an attitude for peace is a necessary condition. Political decisions, treaties, better world structures, and so on, also assume that they are subjectively desired. Peace education intends that many people, on the basis of their own peace attitude, will increasingly want politicians to increasingly want peace.

This describes my intention clearly. It is humble and realistic. The question is not whether sport is functional for peace. That seems to me to be a question that is too ambitious. The realistic question is whether sport education can be functional in the context of peace education.

This does not exclude its having many other goals, including the goal of developing the physical prowess that enables individuals and groups to defend themselves. This does not contradict the aims of peace education, since I have defined peace in a non-utopian way. The idea is not that people should learn to give up the defense of their legitimate interests, nor does it imply an extreme pacifism, e.g., unilateral individual or collective disarmament. This would create situations of such unbalance that aggression would become even more likely. Peace education is not an education for pacifism in this extreme sense. It should teach people that, while defending their own interests, they can be creative in inventing non-violent solutions when their interests conflict with those of others. Precisely because sport interaction is conflictual, it is suited for exercising and reinforcing this creativity.

How can sport education be a fruitful occasion for peace education? What follows is certainly not an exhaustive reply, but rather a form of brainstorming. I will start from four objectives that are constantly cited in the traditional European literature on peace education, and examine then the possibilities sport education has to offer in this regard. These four objectives are: reducing attitudes of militarism, reducing aggressiveness, demolishing enemy images, and development of conflict-solving competence.

Reducing attitudes of militarism

Militarism should not be understood as the readiness to offer legitimate self-defense, which implies the need for an efficient military organization. But a military organization is not necessarily militaristic. Militarism as an attitude means the one-sided faith in problem solving by means of military violence and thus, also, the one-sided promotion of virtues related to the specific goals of that violence: obedience, discipline, courage, and the like. It is the one-sided faith that problem solving in conflict situations is best achieved by the elimination or suppression of the weaker party by means of fighting or war.

Can sport education mean anything here? Apparently, there is precisely a striking analogy between sports and the military. The same virtues, just mentioned, are also important for the sport team. The same language is used: attack, defend, escape, shoot. Historically and anthropologically, sport games can often be interpreted as war rituals or as learning processes for masculine military qualities, or even as physical preparation for the military game. The examples are numerous and are not limited to the Homeric or the medieval knights, or to the sport ideology of Nazism, or times of cold war. The Victorian British sport language was also warlike, and even Coubertin sang in the same choir: "How will the young man acquire manliness. There are only three ways: by war, by love, and by sport. War is the way of former times, the most noble for the individual and perhaps the most useful for the society" (2: p. 196). The matter is relatively innocent insofar as there presently remains only a kind of war metaphor within the semantic of the game ritual. Less innocent is the reversal of the analogy, where war is presented as a game, a supreme game of "strategy, skill and chance" (15). This happens in almost all war films, which are almost always propaganda films to the extent that they conceal violence by using the game analogy.

Now sport education seems to me to be educationally interesting precisely because of these martial analogies, for its task is to bring the truth of the sport game to light. And this truth is that the sport game, however much it has a win-lose structure, still is the structural reverse of the war game. Sport is not "war without weapons," not "war minus the shooting," as George Orwell wrote in The New York Times, in 1959. War is a conflict where the one wins completely and the other loses completely. It is a procedure of conflict resolution by the elimination of the weaker party. Peace is rational conflict resolution so that there are no true losers. In the sport game, there are winners and losers; otherwise, it would not be a sport game and the losers, too, would have no fun. But the losers do not lose themselves. As players, they are not eliminated. They are the players of the next game and have won from the game. Good play education is not so much that which replaces sport by "new games" in which there are no losers, but that which sees to it that the losers are not real losers. By this I mean losers in the social sense of the word, losers of identity and self-respect. Militarism, ultimately, is a danger that threatens education in general. Each teacher, even the mathematics teacher, who plays on competition so that the weaker lose, has a potential militaristic attitude. And good physical education must see to it that the physically less gifted will not experience themselves as "losers" and develop negative body images.

Reducing aggressiveness

This is the only one of the four objectives for which sport is occasionally cited in the literature on peace education. The assumption is that highly competitive and even aggressive play is a relatively safe channeling of inborn aggressive energy, and that therefore, it would reduce the probability of later aggressive acts. This viewpoint is related to the catharsis theory of Konrad Lorenz and others. Many social psychologists, however, do not agree. According to them, aggression is an acquired personality trait and aggressive behavior is learned. Actually, it has not been scientifically demonstrated whether one of the two conceptions embodies the entire truth. In a review by Russell (10), it is shown that some experiments confirm the catharsis function, while others show the opposite. Perhaps, both conceptions reflect part of the truth. It could be that aggression is inborn to a certain extent, but not in the same unambiguous way that we inherit the color of our eyes. Human beings live partially from instinct, but still much more from what is learned. In contrast to the animal, the human being enters the world helpless and relatively instinct-poor. His primary capacity is his capacity to learn. And with aggression there is unmistakably present a learning process that occurs in interaction with the environment. Children learn from their environment. If aggression is not a purely inborn instinct, discharge via sport will not necessarily diminish later aggression in real life. Sport could also be a school for aggressive behavior.

The sport literature that is critical of the catharsis function generally appeals to the well-known counterexamples that have been provided by Sipes (13) and by Sherif (12). Sipes studied 20 tribal societies that were selected because it was unambiguously clear that they had or did not have a warlike character and that combative sports were or were not present. Of the ten very warlike tribes, nine practiced combative sports. Of the ten peaceful tribes, only two knew combative sports. According to the catharsis theory, this situation should be just the reverse. Obviously, such research must be qualified for its scope is very limited. A correlation is not yet a causal explanation. And perhaps these nine tribes would have even more wars if they did not have sport competition. But still, such studies keep us from imagining that sport is automatically functional for the reduction of aggression in real life. The sociologist C.W. Sherif also reported a positive correlation between intergroup aggression and competition. Since her report to the Olympic Congress of Munich in 1972, the experiment is sufficiently well-known in the sport world. It concerned a situation of twelve-year-old boys at a youth camp. When competitions were set up in this homogeneous group, conflicts, severe enmity, and even physical aggression developed. The aggression could not be eliminated by negotiations, by the appointment of a neutral judge, or by the giving of delicious communal meals. The conflict was only resolved by introducing a collective need situation. An artificial drinking water problem was created, so that the boys had to move heaven and earth to get drinking water. However methodologically disputable this experiment might be, the hypothesis is plausible and interesting. Conflict is most efficiently resolved when one finds reason to cooperate. The message for sport is that one may certainly not expect an automatic reduction of aggression. Such a reduction is only possible if a superstructure of cooperative objectives is constructed around it. In this sense, it could be that the Olympic peace discourse, ritually interwoven around sport, is not merely idle rhetoric but hard educational necessity.

Demolishing enemy images

Sociologists know that the acceptance of a negative orientation toward the "out group" can be constitutive for the differentiation of a social group into "in groups" and "out groups." Individuals or groups build their own identity by means of a negative mirror image, "the bad other." Around this image a number of negative stereotypes are constructed, an enemy image against which one can set off one's own identity. Two characteristics are typical of an enemy image. First, it is not necessarily linked with the objectivity of a threat. If there is no true threat, then it is created in an imaginary way. For the enemy is necessary for the sake of one's own identity. And the more horrible the enemy, the closer the cohesion on one's own group. Second, enemy images are almost not falsifiable. They have a built-in mechanism that refutes every refutation. Suppose, for example, that one considers somebody else a very evil person. Should that person suddenly appear to be friendly and helpful, the conclusion tends to be that he is even worse than was thought: he is not only bad but he is also hypocritical. Who knows what he is up to? Festinger has worked out this notion in his theory of cognitive dissonance (5).

Can sport education mean something in the dismantling of enemy images? For the active sport participant, it would seem plausible to assume that he will question a stereotypical enemy image when he comes in contact with players of other nationalities. This assumption, however, seems to have been proven false by many studies. I refer, for example, to the work of the German sociologist H.D. Schmidt, who has specialized in research on nationalistic prejudices and has also involved sport in his research (11). He concludes that prejudices are not automatically eliminated when groups with mutually negative feelings are brought together in games and sport. Two reasons can be given for this. First, the attitude change does not depend on the contact as such, but on the function and the nature of the activity by which the contact is made. Now the sport activity is very antagonistic. It is oriented to the establishment of distinction, and can, therefore, obscure the communal and the binding element between the in group and the out group. And, from my own experience, I know that a number of coaches, even with youth clubs, try to denigrate the opposing team and to stimulate feelings of hate. They use the construction of an enemy image as a stimulus. Second, social perception is insufficient to dislocate enemy images. Our perception of other people follows precisely our orientations and expectations with relation to these people. It tends to exaggerate the behavioral traits that concur with these expectations. Perhaps, in sport, it might also be that when the enemy image is not affected by social perception it offers a better alibi for explaining a possible defeat. When Belgian football teams lose to East European teams, stereotypical explanations emerge: the opponents were poorer players but were perfectly disciplined robots, as you would expect from a collectivistic system. In sport, too, experiences that deviate from prejudicial expectations do not seem to be powerful enough to disturb the mechanism of the enemy image.

Can we be more optimistic with regard to the spectators? Passive sport consumption is important in relation to the problem of the enemy image because here large populations are involved. May one expect that the sport information from the media changes the attitudes of the public toward other nations? Some say yes (9), but there has been as yet no thorough research on the subject, although there is a special commission within the ICSPE on "Sport, Mass Media and International Understanding." This commission has already published a professional code for sport journalists. Halloran, too, of the Center for Mass Communication of the University of Leicester, has compiled a report on the existing literature for this commission. The conclusion of most surveys (6, 8), however, seems to be that no firm conclusions can be drawn. Television, for example, seems to have a very restricted influence on the formation of attitudes toward other nations, and within the television package no influence of sport broadcasts has been demonstrated, neither favorable nor unfavorable. There is no proof of the notion that my image of Russians or Italians would change by the observation of their repeated fair or unfair behavior in televised soccer games. This is not so surprising. Research has shown that, for example, the influence of TV on children is often overestimated. Children are not purely passive recipients of TV images. They interpret them within frameworks that have been created in their education. TV images only have influence if they are reinforced by how things are thought about and discussed in the school and the family. Finally, enemy images are rooted in an entire socio-cultural environment. It is, therefore, very improbable that they will change under the influence of a one-time media event.

Nevertheless, there might be a way of qualifying our skepticism on the basis of an idea that is more intuitive than demonstrable. The more sport is expanded internationally, and for the public at large via the media, the more it may be able to acquire a supra-national image. Athletes would then no longer simply represent a nation, but a kind of supra-national sport culture with its own code and value scale that break away from nationalistic enemy images. Thus, McIntosh suggests that certain athletes like Owens, Bikila, or Bannister have, in fact, transcended their own nationality (8: p. 280). Finally, it is promising that a Russian sport poll sponsored by Tass, selected the American swimmer Debbie Myers as sportswoman of the year in 1967, at the height of the Vietnam War. Here we touch the heart of the Olympic ideology, which rests on the fundamental hypothesis that internationalism leads to supra-nationalism.

Development of conflict-solving competence

Such competition implies the acceptance of conflicts and the capacity to handle them non-violently. Educators recommend role playing as an efficient strategy to learn how to make compromises, to accept arbitration, and so on. But, of course, such role playing already exists in the sport game. Play, as Sutton-Smith has convincingly demonstrated (14), is "information processing." It is a learning process whereby members of a group adapt to the values of that group. In competitive games, players learn how to behave in conflict situations with an uncertain outcome. It is not by chance that modern sport arose in England. It is the role playing of the modern democratic society that found its first expression in England with John Locke.

Its basic idea is the acceptance of the mixed character of social life. Totalitarianism understands society as a uniform totality. Democracy is based on the multiplicity of individuals, on their differentiation. The society is conceived on the basis of the idea of a contract whereby individuals delegate authority and agree on all sorts of procedures for decision making when opinions differ. The intention is not to suppress differences in an urge to achieve consensus. That something like voting is provided in parliament means a recognition of the difference.

Democracy is a kind of game, the sticking to agreed upon game rules in decision making. The authentic game is, therefore, the appropriate "information processing" for this. One learns to accept opposition, to make agreements on procedures (the rules of the game), to respect them (fairness), to delegate authority (the referee), to subject oneself to whatever the result is of the accepted procedures (to be a good loser). In short, one acquires peace competence. For one learns how to deal with opposition by means of agreed upon procedures (4: pp. 263-265). Or as Coubertin expressed it: "It is childish to demand that people love each other. But it is not utopian to demand that they respect each other" (3: p. 133). It is striking, however, that this statement was made in a speech entitled Pax Olympica, which was given over Berlin radio in 1935 and was published by the Organizing Committee of the Olympic Games of Berlin in 1936.

The great French philosopher and sociologist Raymond Aron expressed a similar idea in a text that he wrote over the world soccer championships in Spain, 1982: "Let us not be ironic over this great feast, not of friendship but of competition between the nations. Subjecting competition to rules supervised by referees, is this not the picture of the only conceivable reconciliation between peoples that is compatible with the nature of communities and perhaps of the person himself" (1)?

Possible negative effects

Good education must also be concerned about the possible negative side-effects of the means employed. I want to offer here for consideration the principal danger that arises from the varied character of sport. Sport interactions are both associative and conflictual, cooperative and competitive. This conflictual content is very high, and this for two reasons. First, the conflict is not purely indirect. This would mean that opponents fight for the same prize with efforts that occur in parallel. They would then not interfere directly with each other. An example of indirect conflict is economic market competition. In sport, the conflict is also direct. A good performance often means that one has succeeded in hindering the opponent in his play (4: p. 261).

Second, sport embodies a very special type of opposition, namely what sociological jargon calls "inconclusive competition." In conclusive competition one only wants to know who won the game here and now (e.g., a Miss World contest). Sport games, however, are never concluded. The ending of today's game is the beginning of tomorrow's. The winner sets new norms and new performance levels. The losers of today have to surpass these levels if, tomorrow, they want to have a chance of winning. And the winner, in his turn, must accept this challenge if he still wants to be considered the winner tomorrow. This creates a spiral of continuous shifting of performance norms and of the drive to succeed. And this spiral endangers the four objectives of peace education I have given. In particular, it could threaten the democratic capacity of sport from within. The Finnish sport sociologist Heinilä calls this the threat of totalization (7). This implies two things. First, the effort of the individual no longer suffices to meet the compelled performance level. All available means must be employed, and for this the total social system must be mobilized: economy, education, technology, scientific research. Thus, oppositions (e.g., East-West) are not dismantled but rather reinforced. The athlete represents only a social system.

Second, totalization also occurs inwardly. Athletes become only pawns of a system (a club, an organization, a nation). Totalitarian pressure on the individual increases. In crisis situations, a group tends to totalization, in equilibrium situations more to democratization. Now, inconclusive competition is to be seen as a permanent situation of tension or crisis. The danger of totalizing pressure or violence on the individual is, therefore, structurally present in sport, particularly where great size, internationalism, media publicity, etc., generate the increasing drive to succeed. Good sport education must be aware of this danger. Only one who is so aware can resolve the danger. Under this condition, the close human interaction that marks sport can be a powerful opportunity in education for those who want to promote attitudes of peace.

Conclusion

And perhaps this educator may offer one last consideration. It could be that in sport still richer capabilities are involved than those I have mentioned here. Indeed, I have worked with a very realistic definition of peace. I defined this notion not as a conflict-free situation but as a situation where people have conflict-solving skills. Indeed, it would be wonderful if people could cope with conflicts in a reasonable manner.

And sport education can teach this. But in our hearts we long for a peace that is still richer than that--a paradise of universal equality, solidarity, and fraternity. This is precisely the theological concept of peace. I have called this utopian because its direct achievement in history is not possible. Still, it is an ideal that can provide an important degree of dynamism to each concrete striving for peace. And, perhaps, this dynamic can be experienced under the surface of sport itself. Perhaps sport can contribute not only to the acceptance of opposition and procedures. Perhaps there is room for other experiences. We should be able to learn more from it than how to cope with conflicts in a reasonable way. We learn also that performance is brief and fame ephemeral. We learn how capacities are developed to the point of failure, as in high jumping. We learn that we all share in losing. And we discover that, in this human inadequacy and deficiency, we are more essentially equal than unequal in the winning.

Leuven, Belgium

BIBLIOGRAPHY

1. Aron, R. "Confession d'un fan." L'Express, 16 April 1982, 67.

2. Coubertin, P. Essais de psychologie sportive. Lausanne: Payot, 1913.

3. _____. L'idee Olympique. Discours et essais. Schorndorf: Hofmann, 1967.

4. De Wachter, F. "Are Sports a Factor for Peace?" In Topical Problems of Sport Philosophy. Edited by H. Lenk. Schorndorf: Hofmann, 1983.

5. Festinger, L. A Theory of Cognitive Dissonance. Stanford, CA: Stanford University, 1966.

6. Halloran, J.D. Mass Media, Sport and International Understanding. A Summary of a Review of Literature and Research. London: ICSPE, 1981.

7. Heinilä, K. The Totalization Process in International Sport. Jyvaskyla: University of Jyvaskyla, 1982.

8. McIntosh, P.C. "International Communication, Sport and International Understanding." In Sport and International Understanding. Edited by M. Ilmarinen. Berlin-Heidelberg-New York-Tokyo: Springer, 1984.

9. Milhstein, O.A., Molchanov, S.V. "The Shaping of Public Opinion Regarding Sport by the Mass Media as a Factor Promoting International Understanding." International Review of Sport Sociology, 1976, 3, 71-85.

10. Russel, G.W. "Psychological Issues in Sports Aggression." In Sports Violence. Edited by J.H. Goldstein. New York: Springer, 1983.

11. Schmidt, H.D. "Sport und Vorurteile, insbesondere national-istische Einstellungen." In Soziale Einflusse im Sport. Edited by D. Bierhoff-Alfermann. Darmstadt: D. Steinkopf, 1976.

12. Sherif, C.W. "Intergroup Conflict and Competition." In Sport in the Modern World--Chances and Problems. Edited by O. Grupe et al., Berlin-Heidelberg-New York: Springer, 1973.

13. Sipes, R. "War, Sports and Aggression: An Empirical Test of Two Theories." The American Anthropologist, 1973, vol. 75, 64-86.

14. Sutton-Smith, B. "Games, the Socialization of Conflict." In Sport in the Modern World--Chances and Problems. Edited by O. Grupe et al., Berlin-Heidelberg-New York: Springer, 1973.

15. Veitch, C.R. "Play Up! Play Up! And Win the War! The Propaganda of Athleticism in Britain, 1914-1918." In Sport and Politics. Edited by G. Redmond. Champaign, IL: Human Kinetics Pub., 1984.

THE SPIRIT OF THE CELTS IN SPORT

by Sean Egan

There are few races in Europe who do not have Celtic blood. The French and the Germans are partially Celtic. Britain was first ruled by Celts. The Britonic branch of the Celtic people were in Britain when the Romans arrived there. The six distinctive areas where the Celts settled down and left a lasting legacy are Brittany in France, Wales, Cornwall in Southern England, the Isle of Man, the Highlands of Scotland and Ireland. Each group developed over time its own version of the Celtic tongue. The Irish Gaelic, Scottish Gaelic, and Manx made up the Gaelic branch of the language, and Breton, Welsh and Cornish made up the Britonic branch of the language. Manx and Cornish are no longer spoken. Reading through this article you will become aware that the Celtic tongue was a very strong part of the Celtic culture. Over time the Celts have emigrated to many countries throughout the world and have taken with them their distinctive spirit for life, language, music, games and fun.

I was born a Celt in a small village on the extreme west coast of the island of Eire (Ireland). For one quarter of a century I was steeped in the Celtic traditions and ways. In school, we spoke only Gaelic. We played only Gaelic games, sung only Gaelic songs and danced reels, jigs and hornpipes. Our school books were filled with stories and poems about the Celtic heroes of ancient Ireland who were so proud of their heritage and culture that they fought hard and often died to protect and preserve it. Our teachers were somewhat fanatical about our history, freedom, culture and games. They preached and lived by their preaching, and we were their staunch followers. We learned to revere everything Irish. For those of us who had a serious problem learning the Gaelic tongue, school life was difficult. Elementary school was a training ground where our young minds, energies and spirits were harnessed and molded to express the spirit of the Celts through language, sport, music, dance and fun. We loved it. School was not a dull place. This was to be the only schooling for most of us. We never moved outside a radius of ten miles until we were fourteen years old. We grew up in an environment of contrasts: poverty and beauty, peace and violence, abstinence from alcohol and drunkenness. Regardless of their faults and failures, the Irish as I knew them were a very proud people. They were proud of their ancient and modern warriors. They were proud of their language, music, games, and religion. The Irish or Gaels of the past valued above everything else beauty of person and courage in battle (21). Their poems and sagas constantly celebrate these virtues. They were a tall race, fair haired or red haired, with white skin and blue or green eyes. The old Celts loved to do battle, and when they were not busy fighting against the enemy, they fought among themselves.

The spirit of the Celts has been manifested in many ways. Religion, politics, language and games are all closely mingled and intertwined. In this article I will dwell mostly on the Celtic spirit as manifested by their games.

My own background and experience will flavor the analysis and, we hope, help the reader to gain an insight into the spirit of the Celts in sport.

Even though there are six Celtic groups mentioned, only three major groups of games have been seriously developed and studied: the Tailteann games of ancient Ireland, the Gaelic Athletic games (G.A.A.) of modern Ireland, and the Highland games of Scotland. Mention will also be made of such activities as Cornish hurling and Breton wrestling.

The Tailteann Games

This was a collection of games and athletic activities performed by the Celts of ancient Ireland. According to legend, it was instituted by Lugh Lamh Fada (Lugh of the long arm) in commemoration of his foster mother Tailte (13). Mention of the games has been made in many of the old Irish history books (22); (8); (17). Tailte's husband was King Eocaidh Mac Erc,

36

the last Firbolg monarch of Ireland. He was killed at the battle of Moytura in County Mayo, in 1896 B.C. (22). This battle was preceded by a fierce hurling match between two teams of 27 each. The casualties were buried under a huge cairn (4). Such dating, if accurate, would, of course, place these games centuries before the first Olympic games in Greece.

These games were known as funeral games and were part of a bigger gathering known as the Aonach Tailteann. The function of the games was, first, to do honor to the illustrious dead; secondly, to promote laws, and thirdly, to entertain the people. In addition to athletic contests, there were competitions for craftsmen, jewelers, goldsmiths, weavers, dyers, spinners and makers of shields and implements of war. It was also a time for trading and commercial transactions (18). The games consisted of athletic, gymnastic and equestrian contests of various kinds, and included running, long-jumping, high-jumping, hurling, quoit throwing, spear casting, spear or pole vaulting, sword and shield contests, wrestling, boxing, swimming, horse racing, chariot racing, sling contests and bow and arrow exhibitions. In addition, there were literacy, musical, oratorical and story-telling competitions, singing and dancing competitions (10); (17). There were prescribed by-laws for the games (18). Similar by-laws were instituted and enforced at Olympia (3). All feuds, fights, quarrels and similar disturbances were strictly forbidden. It was a fair without sin, fraud, insult, theft, contention or rude hostility (16). A universal truce was proclaimed in the High King's name, and "woe betide the man who broke it" (22). Women were not excluded from the assembly (as was the case at Olympia). Special features were provided to attract women to the gathering such as a match-making mart and marriage ceremony. A particular enclosure called the Cot, or Cotha, was provided for the exclusive use of women.

The Tailteann games were also an established recruiting centre and testing station, which Fionn Mac Cool regularly attended with his officers to test all those who wished to join his famous army, the Fianna Eireann. Fionn, who lived and died in the third century of the Christian era, was one of the greatest athletic figures of Irish history (12).

This festival was an important part of Irish life up to the Norman invasion of Ireland in 1169, when it declined as a major festival, but it continued until about 1830 as a local gathering. The games were revived in 1924, just after Irish independence from Britain. This was a time when the Irish people as a whole were searching for their roots in pre-history. The festival was again repeated in 1928 and 1932 but thereafter disappeared (23). Joyce (12) sums up the spirit of the ancient games in the following phrase: "...these beautiful days of jubilee provided for a highly sociable and gregarious, but clannish and quick-tempered, people who equally loved sporting and battling, the matching of power in games, civil or warlike." These lines skillfully depict part of the Celtic spirit. The 1924 revival spread over a 16-day period. One celebrated not only the most popular pastimes, but also literature, sculpture, music, several forms of aquatic and equine sport, chess, dancing, golf, tennis, billards and even air racing (2).

The modern Tailteann games were held in 1963. They were known as the Willwood Junior Tailteann Festival. The objectives of the Willwood Tailteann Foundation were: (1) to encourage the Tailteann ideal amongst the youth of the country by organizing annually a festival of sport and cultural activities, and (2) to promote the Tailteann Movement in Ireland by encouraging public and governmental support for the renewal of the Aonach Tailteann as a National Festival. These modern games have been held every year, since 1963, in Ireland and are increasing in both size and scope (15). There is also an annual cycle race held in Ireland each year called "Ras Tailteann" which attracts some of the best cyclists in the world.

Highland Games of Scotland

The Highland games, sometimes referred to as the Highland Gatherings, date back to 1080 A.D. (29). King Malcolm III organized a contest at Braemar Castle to find "a man fleet of foot and of good stamina to convey the royal dispatches safely to Edinburgh." The race was run uphill to the summit of Craig Choinnich. This was the beginning of the Highland games. The event lasted until 1380, when the Black Death had emptied Braemar of its population. The games were revived for a brief time. (The date is uncertain.) They were banned after the defeat of Bonnie Prince Charles in 1746.

The ancient Highland Gatherings consisted of dancing, piping and athletic events (31). Much pomp and ritual was attached to the games. Officials were often Druids, so that a solemnity and auspicious sanction prevailed in the early contests (5). Competitors marched through the arena to the sound of music. Many Scottish games included marshalled pipe bands and the tossing of a long wooden pole called a caber (5). According to Webster (31), the first event of the program was a game of shinty, which is similar to hurling (4). Twenty-four strapping warriors with carved sticks took the field and began to chase a horse hair ball. They were divided into two teams and were intent on beating the ball over the line on their opponents' part of the field. This was followed by a chariot race. At the games, the ground was divided into sections. While the wrestlers and jumpers competed at one side of the arena, hammer throwers and stone putters threw in another section. Archery and sling shooting were also part of the games. The old folk were not forgotten, and for them harpists played, sang and recited stories of the days gone by (31). Legend has it that the clan chiefs would hold competitions to pick the strongest men as bodyguards and the fastest as couriers, thus giving the games a military function similar to that of the Tailteann games.

The modern games were revived in 1832 (31). There were five events and a prize of five pounds for the winner of each event. This made the games professional games. In 1865, the Prince of Wales visited Braemar. The events contested were "tossing the caber, the hill race, throwing the hammer, putting the stone, sword dancing, bagpipe music, translating Gaelic, flat racing (200-2000 yards), the high leaps, the long jump, the sack race and the hurdle race" (26). This indicated the wide scope of interests of the Celts. The athletic events of the modern games often consisted of heavy events, light events and novelty events. The heavy events were: putting the stone for distance (56 lbs); hammer throw for distance; weight toss for height over a bar (56 lbs); sheaf toss for height over a bar; caber toss for accuracy (no standard size). The light events consisted of running and jumping contests whereas the novelty items changed from place to place and from year to year. Some of the common novelty events were tug o'war, pillow fights, lifting heavy stones and climbing greasy poles.

According to Webster (31) the Highland games have been incorporated into international athletics. Redmond (28) notes that the Scottish pastimes were a significant influence in the development of American track and field. The hammer throw, the pole-vault, and shot-putting were Caledonian in origin.

Emigration was responsible for the spread of the games to other countries, in particular the U.S.A. and Canada (28). In Scotland there are 78 games yearly and there is an upsurge of the games in Japan, Hawaii, Indonesia, Australia, New Zealand, Greece, Sweden's Isle of Gotland, Iceland, and of course, the U.S.A. and Canada (5).

Modern Gaelic Games

The modern Gaelic games were revived and organized by Michael Cusack when he founded the Gaelic Athletic Association (G.A.A.) in 1884 (2). The G.A.A. is the largest and most popular association in Irish sport today. It concentrates its energies in the promotion of Gaelic football and hurling. The purpose of the G.A.A. is to preserve and promote native Irish games (1). Hurling, Gaelic football and handball (since 1924), along with women's camogie (since 1904), are the games that come within the scope of the G.A.A.'s influence. Road bowls and rounders are also played by a minority in Ireland but are not a major concern of the G.A.A.

Hurling is Ireland's national game. It is a game of skill and speed, one of the fastest team games in the world. It is played by a fifteen-a-side team using hurling sticks and a small leather ball called a sliothar. Scoring is either by a goal or a point. A goal equals three points. When the sliothar is hit over the crossbar and between the goal posts, a point is scored. When the ball goes under the crossbar, a goal is scored.

Camogie is the women's version of hurling. Its beginnings are due to the women's section of the Gaelic League--the National language movement. We must remember that these were not just games, they were Gaelic games that were specific to a people, its culture and language.

40

Gaelic football is Ireland's most popular game. It is a unique game in that it seems to have no connection in its formation with similar football games (1). The earliest reference to ball games (aside from hurling) in Ireland is the Statutes of Galway, 1537, which forbade "hurling and all other ball games" (27). The poet MacCurta, writing in 1660, describes a game that clearly included snatching and carrying of a ball (1). This was the original Gaelic football. Gaelic football as played today, looks like a mixture of soccer and rugby skills. The ball is round like a soccer ball. Players are allowed to handle the ball but are not allowed to pick it off the ground by hand. The ball must be collected from the ground using the tip of the toe. Carrying the ball is allowed when one bounces, hops, or passes it from toe back to hand. Scoring is similar to hurling. Tripping, tackling above the knee, and wrestling features of the old game are no longer permitted. The old style kick and rush football game gave way to the catch and kick style which is the basis of the modern Gaelic football game. Currently the game demands more skill and is less aggressive.

The Irish Handball Council, with the support of the G.A.A., was set up in 1924 (2). Irish handball is a game played by individuals or doubles in a four-walled court similar to a squash court. The game is terminated when one player scores 21 points. Two types of balls are used, a soft-ball and a hard-ball. The soft-ball games are more popular and are played extensively in Ireland and abroad. The hard-ball game is played only in Ireland (14).

The Gaelic Athletic Association (G.A.A.) was founded "for the preservation and cultivation of national pastimes" (27). Its founder, Michael Cusack, was a man of quick and impulsive temper, not given to easy cooperation. He dreamed and worked for a Gaelic Ireland, true to itself and to its inheritance in language, games, recreation, pastimes and moral standards as he knew them. He had developed a consuming passion for true amateurism and a horror of every vice associated with rigged sports, especially betting, roping, book-running, dishonest handicapping, selective programming, and so on. He despised elitism and fought for the equality of all men in sport regardless of class or creed (19). Cusack had a unusual affection for the Gaelic language, and according to his own testimony, the

G.A.A. was born out of the language. An "Anglicized G.A.A. is a contradiction," Cusack was known to say (19).

Archbishop Croke was one of the co-founders of the G.A.A. He saw sport as a means towards building up the morale of those who participated in competition. Through his influence many of the priests became involved in organizing Gaelic games at the parish level. As a Nationalist, Croke saw the G.A.A. as one part of an overall attempt to achieve Irish Independence. Croke believed that the G.A.A. for the Ireland of his day (under British rule) offered a spirit of Democracy in a sphere of activity (games) where hitherto an English hand ruled (30). He believed also that the G.A.A. might help eliminate Ireland of one of its greatest scourges--emigration. Having lived for so many years as an exile, Croke noted: "I've seen the scattered children of our race in almost every land that the sun shines upon...I've no hesitation whatsoever in saying that an Irishman's fittest and happiest home is in Ireland..." (30). Croke was much concerned about the moral side-issues of sport, such as missing mass and excessive drinking. He proposed that no alcohol be sold in or near the athletic fields; that sporting venues not be near public houses, and that no prizes be accepted from publicans. He also suggested no games on Sunday.

According to O'Tuathaigh (25), the central ideas on which the G.A.A. was founded were: the affirmation of an independent and democratic ideal in sport and a clear statement of a version of Irish cultural autonomy. The Irish were always lovers of freedom and spent 800 years trying to achieve it at an ultimate cost for many. To have an idea of how radical the founding of the G.A.A. was in the post-famine years, one has only to recall the political state of Ireland at that time. Between 1851-1911, two million people left Ireland; traditional customs, pastimes, religious customs, as well as sport and leisure activities were abandoned. The famine of 1847, the emigration of youth, bankrupt landlords, pauperising poor-laws, grinding officials and demoralizing workhouses had broken somewhat the spirit of the people. Sullivan wrote in 1877: "Their ancient sports and pastimes everywhere disappeared and in many parts...have never returned. The outdoor games, the hurling match...are seen no more" (25). The British government availed of the opportunity to intensify the Anglicisation of the island.

Croke, one of the co-founders of the G.A.A., noted a few years after the founding of the G.A.A. that:

> ball-playing, hurling, foot-ball, kicking according to Irish rules, leaping in various ways, wrestling, hand-grips, top-pegging, leap-frog, rounders, tip-in-the-hat, and all such favorite exercises and amusements amongst men and boys may now be said to be not only dead and buried, but in several localities to be entirely forgotten and unknown (25).

Irish athletics were completely controlled by the British athletics authorities. It was against this background that Cusack and his colleagues founded the G.A.A. Davin, who was the third co-founder member of the G.A.A., is regarded as the Father of Modern Irish Athletics. His concern was to preserve the dignity and vindicate the prestige of native athleticism and preserve it from humiliating alien influences (6).

This organization was responsible for the preservation of Gaelic games; it stimulated local leadership and it involved the priest in community life through sport. It was nationalist in spirit. It was a strong proponent for an independent, united Ireland in 1884. Today it denounces the violence in Northern Ireland but still aspires to a united Ireland (20). The G.A.A. personifies the spirit of a phoenix people who rose against all odds from the ashes to flourish and shine today (103 years later), not only in every country, village, and parish, but in every hamlet in the remotest parts of Ireland. There are 8,000 Gaelic clubs in Ireland alone and many more clubs in cities all over the world where the Irish have settled. This is a tribute to the fighting spirit of the Irish who consistently and without fail laboured to be themselves: lovers of freedom, democratic, proud of their heritage and country, Gaelic, spiritual and idealistic. Scrutinizing carefully the Gaelic personality, one finds that the Joycean image of the loud-voiced, hard-drinking, anti-English, war-hungry braggart is not very accurate. Such a description may be true for a minority of the population, but such characters are present in most societies. Puirseal (27) says about the G.A.A.: "The extraordinary growth of this one humble enough association is really a measure of the vitality that lies inert in the common people...In spirit as in its achievement it is not only unique but astonishing." And MacMahon (11) states that "the G.A.A., in the idiom of self-reliance, joy, dignity, spectacle and achievement, has more that vindicated our traditional claim to nationhood."

While the populations of all the developed countries in the Western World have been steadily declining in recent years, the Irish population has known a sharp increase. Thirty-nine point six percent (39.6%) of the population is under 19 years. This young nation has been exposed to many outside influences, particularly T.V. and radio. Youth have been exposed to other games, such as soccer, rugby, field hockey, and so on. A census taken in 1971 (24) indicated that: 47% of urban and 82.3% of rural students liked football; 54.1% of rural students liked hurling; 63% of rural and 35.5% of urban students liked handball. The study also indicated that 58% of young people were inter-ested in Gaelic games and 42% of young people played these games. In secondary school, 72% of the students are involved in Gaelic games, while 84% of vocational schools get involved in these games. In Ireland today youth play most games. This was not always the case. Some years ago the G.A.A. rescinded its so called "Ban" rule. This rule forbade people from competing in Gaelic games if they played a foreign game such as rugby or soccer.

Modern Ireland has many world class runners, cyclists, rugby and soccer players, boxers, equestrian riders and field hockey players (9). The Irish athletes are admired all over the world for their tenacity and fighting spirit. They often buttress what they lack in skill with a "never give up will-power." This was aptly shown by John Treacy's silver medal win in the marathon of the 1984 Olympics, Sean Kelly's high ranking in the Tour de France of 1982, the N. Ireland soccer team's placing in the 1982 World Cup, and Barry McGuigan's climb to be a World featherweight champion. Like Barry, I dreamed of being a World Champion in boxing and devoted ten years of hard work to the grueling training of the "noble art of self-defense." Ironically, today I spend as much energy trying to ban boxing in its present format. Due to the serious brain damage and fatalities caused in boxing, I advocate a non-con-tact-to-the-head boxing. Boxing had its origins in the funeral games where sometimes the competitors fought to the death.

This very primitive sport, which had its origins in the primitive funeral games, has no place in our civilized society in its present format. The primitive instincts of man can be channeled in this sport, while at the same time avoiding serious damages if the head is removed from the target-striking zone. As one of the "fighting Irish" and as a Celt, I have no hesitation in advocating the abolition of boxing in its present format. Even so, I must admit I did enjoy boxing while competing at the national and international level over a ten-year period. However, I never suffered any serious damage, and perhaps, I was one of the lucky ones.

Boxing has always been held in great prestige among the Irish. It symbolized their struggle for freedom and is linked closely with the spirit of the old Celt. It is true that emotions will oftentimes surmount logic in matters dealing with national symbols. Such is the case with many of our Celts with regards to boxing.

This article would not be complete if mention was not made of a few other sports played by the Celts such as Cornish hurling. It differed fundamentally from Irish hurling and the hurling (shinty) played by the Gaels of Scotland. Sticks were not used. There were two variants: hurling to goals, where a small ball was carried or thrown through the adversaries' goal and "hurling to the country" where the ball was brought homewards through the countryside. There was also Breton wrestling or gouren. In gouren one fights in a standing position only. The aim is to throw one's adversary. The two wrestlers grip each other's shirts (specially made) in various holds and use legs to throw them off balance. A lamm, or a throw in which one's adversary lands squarely on his two shoulders is sought. Matches are timed and a point system determines winners. Before each fight there is the traditional hand shake. The motto of these wrestlers is: Gwary wheag yu gwary teag ("Good play is fair play").

To conclude and sum up this brief analysis of the spirit of the Celts in sport, I should mention that over the past two decades there has been a dramatic revival of Celtic language, music and games. The University of Ottawa established a Celtic Chair in 1985 and many North American universities teach courses in the Gaelic language. Cornish and Manx are also undergoing a revival. Breton wrestling recently made its North American debut.

The Celts are an outgoing, gregarious, quick-tempered people who love "sporting and battling." They are lovers of freedom and fair-play and will go to all kinds of extremes to achieve them. Courageous to the end, they will die rather than give up. Like steel that is put through fire, the Celts survived the ordeals of hardship and oppression and became stronger and more determined. More than anything else, the Celts cherish freedom. They wish to be free to practice their own customs, religion, games, music and dance.

Ottawa, Ontario

46

BIBLIOGRAPHY

1. Carroll, N. Sport in Ireland. Dublin: Department of Foreign Affairs (Cahill Printers Ltd.).

2. de Burca, M. The G.A.A. A History of the Gaelic Athletic Association. Dublin: Cumann Luthcleas Gael, 1980.

3. Drees, L. Olympia: Gods, Artists and Athletes. London: Pall Mall Press, 1968.

4. Eriu, vol. viii, 1915, p. 29.

5. Fales, D.A. Highland Games Sketchbook. Ottawa: Borealis Press, 1982.

6. G.A.A. A Century of Service 1884-1984. Dublin: Croke Park, 1984.

G.A.A. A Century of Service 1884-1984. Dublin: Cumann Luthcleas Gael, 1984.

8. Keating, G. History of Ireland From the Earliest Period to the English Invasion, Trans., John O'Mahony. New York: P.M. Haverty, 1857.

9. Logan, M. Irish Sport. Dublin: The O'Brien Press, 1983.

10. MacAuliffe, M.J. The History of Aonach Tailteann and the Ancient Irish Laws. National Library of Ireland, 1928.

11. MacMahon, B. The G.A.A.: A Sense of Place. G.A.A. 1884-1984. Siompoisiam An Cheid. Colaiste na hOllscoile Corcaigh, 1984.

12. MacManus, S. The Story of the Irish Race. New York: Irish Publishing Co., 1922.

13. MacNeill, M. The Festival of Lughnasa - A study of the survival of the Celtic festival of the beginning of the harvest. Oxford: Oxford University Press, 1862.

14. McElligott, T. Handball. Dublin: Wolfhound Press, 1984.

15. McKernan, M. A Historical Account of the Three Phases of Aonach Tailteann. Unpublished Master's Thesis, Springfield College, 1981.

16. Metrical dindseanchas, Part IV, "Tailtu," Trans. Ed. Gwynn. Hodges and Figgus Co., Ltd., 1924, pp. 147-167.

17. Murphy, D. Short History of Ireland. Dublin: Fallon and Co., Ltd., 1894.

18. Nally, T.H. The Aonach Tailteann and the Tailteann Games: Their origin, history and ancient associations. Dublin: Talbot Press, Ltd., 1922.

19. O'Caithnia, L. Croke, Cusack and Davin: The Founders. G.A.A. 1884-1984. Siompoisiam An Cheid. Colaiste na hOllscoile. Corcaigh, 1984.

20. O'Ciardha, T. Challenges of Tomorrow. G.A.A. 1884-1984. Siomposiam An Cheid. Colaiste na Hollscoile. Corcaigh, 1984.

21. O'Connor, U. Irish Tales and Sagas. London: Granada Publishing, 1981.

22. O'Donovan, J. Annals of the Kingdom of Ireland by the Four Masters from the Earliest Period to the Year 1616. Dublin: Hodges and Smith, 1851.

23. O'Hanlon & Robinson. Aonach Tailteann, Memorandum and Articles of Association. Dublin, 1932.

24. O'Mailmhichil, L. Youth and the G.A.A. G.A.A. 1884-1984. Siompoisiam An Cheid. Colaiste na hOllscoile. Corcaigh, 1984.

25. O'Tuathaigh, G. The G.A.A.: A Movement of National

Consequences - An Historical Perspective. G.A.A. 1884-1984. Siompoisiam An Cheid. Colaiste na hOllscoile. Corcaigh, 1984.

26. Powell, T. The Game: The Marshall Cavendish Encyclopedia of World Sports. XLVII. London: Marshall Cavendish, Ltd., 1970.

27. Puirseal, P. The G.A.A. in its Time. Dublin: Ward River Press, 1984.

28. Redmond, G. Caledonian Games and American Track and Field in the Nineteenth Century. World Symposium on the History of Physical Education and Sport. Banff, 1971.

29. Solberg, S. "The Highland Games," JOPHER, Nov./Dec. 1974, pp. 19-21.

30. Tierney, M. Croke, Cusack & Davin: The Founders. G.A.A. 1884-1984. Siompoisiam An Cheid. Colaiste na hOllscoile. Corcaigh, 1984.

31. Webster, D. Scottish Highland Games. Edinburgh: MacDonald Printers Ltd., 1973.

SPECIAL OLYMPICS--SPORT IN THE PUREST FORM

by Michele Gelfman

If someone were to ask me to explain the importance of Special Olympics, my first inclination would be to describe it in terms of handicapped individuals learning to believe in themselves and (conversely) our coming to believe in them. Every so often in our lifetime we encounter a person who alters our perception of life. For me, she was a little girl in the Special Olympics.

I was introduced to her along with the other Special Olympians who were to compete in the tennis event. It seemed evident from the skill test that she would not do as well as most of the other participants. As Director, I assigned the most qualified person to assist her prior to the events. There existed a time limit for each category in the skill test, and, after several skills, I went to check on the little girl's progress.

She had only hit a few balls correctly, so I stood behind her and physically helped her hit. When she pulled away from me, I was somewhat taken aback, especially when she said, "You know, I can do it myself!" And, she proved to everyone that she could. She did not finish with the lowest score in the event and afterwards she went running to my assistant proclaiming, "I did it. I did it." At that moment I realized that my personal standards of perfection in my own game were transmitted to the same standards which she has strived for, but at a different level. If anything, it was a humbling experience. There are no words to convey the pride and enthusiasm of that moment. You have to experience it to understand it.

That's why the Special Olympics is, indeed, so special. In a world where so many things we experience are tainted by money, prestige, and power, there is a glow of purity, honesty, and enjoyment about this event. The values associated with it are unique.

53

My involvement with Special Olympics has been on the State and International levels. The feeling is like nothing I've ever experienced. Happiness, sadness, frustration and exuberance are all part of the ultimate goal--not winning, per se, but accomplishment! The training, the hard work, the desire to succeed, comes, in my view, from three main facets: heart, dedication, and integrity. The Special Olympians have exhibited, through the support of coaches, parents, family, and friends, a sense of being and pride that can easily bring tears to anyone's eyes. They can proudly say: "I am special. I am important." But, most of all, they can say, "I am loved!" This marvelous program has been established worldwide. The physical training and athletic competition was created in 1968 by the Joseph P. Kennedy, Jr., Foundation. Now approximately 20,000 athletes in communities around the world test their skills each year.[1]

To understand the Special Olympics fully we must go back to the origin and creation of this remarkable program. As with all great accomplishments, the Special Olympics began simply with a need, a plan, and people with enough conviction to make a dream a reality.

In June of 1963, Eunice Kennedy Shriver started a day-care camp in her home for mentally retarded individuals. Her goal was to explore the capabilities of these children and adults in a variety of sports and physical activities. The idea caught fire. Under the sponsorship of the Joseph P. Kennedy, Jr., Foundation, summer day camps and the athletes they served blossomed across the country and inspired hundreds of groups to form Special Olympics programs on local, state, and regional levels. The results were astounding! Mentally retarded athletes who had heard "You can't do it," all their lives, proved that they could, if they only had the chance.

In 1968, five short years later, Mrs. Shriver organized the first International Special Olympics in Chicago's Soldier Field. Nearly one thousand athletes from the United States and Canada participated.

The early 1970's marked a period of impressive milestones for Special Olympics. All fifty states now had organizations and state directors. Special Olympic Games were held in France, the first notable participation outside North America. New events were added. National media networks began broadcasting Special Olympics competition; national sports associations officially supported Special Olympics events, such as basketball and floor hockey.

The International Special Olympics games are now held every four years. The first International Winter Special Olympics, held in 1977, attracted hundreds of athletes as well as major network coverage. Participation grew on all levels. In 1983, the Sixth International Summer Special Olympics were held at Louisiana State University, in Baton Rouge, Louisiana. The Games drew 4,000 athletes bearing flags from more than 50 nations. Sixty thousand spectators witnessed the opening ceremonies. Twenty-three thousand people volunteered their time as coaches, organizers, guides, timers, or simply as "huggers," who welcome athletes across the finish line.

The theme for the 1987 International Games is "A Time for Heroes." It will be like nothing you've ever seen before. There will be little feeling of nation-pitted-against nation. There will be no contracts or endorsements. The athletes will celebrate their victories over the only thing they want to beat, the odds. At the conclusion of the Special Olympics, everyone leaves a winner, for what they prize is not victory alone, but the reward which comes with courageous effort.

During the ten days of the International Games, more than 4,000 talented, trained athletes from around the world and across the nation will gather to show the world what great strength of character and athletic skill they possess.

Special Olympics is a never-ending story of personal courage on the part of the athletes and selfless giving by volunteers who've been there every step of the way. Yet, the milestones that have been reached will be exceeded as the story continues in 1987. At the 1987 Summer Games, Civitan International, a 55,000 member volunteer service organization, will continue its long tradition of support and become the first officially recognized "premiere" sponsor of the 1987 International Summer Olympics Games with a pledge of $1.6 million.

There is no "typical" Special Olympian. They are of different ages, from across town to across the world. They are quiet heroes who have triumphed over unasked-for handicaps; people who, by example, enrich the lives of everyone they meet. They do, however, share one crucial trait—a competitive fire to do their personal best. They will come to the International Games to compete in eight official sports, including aquatics (swimming and diving), athletics (track and field, wheelchair events and frisbee), basketball, bowling, gymnastics, soccer, softball, and volleyball. Demonstration events include road cycling, equestrian events, roller skating, tennis, table tennis, and weight lifting. Special Olympics accommodates competitors at all ability levels by assigning them to division based on age and actual performance. Nearly one million mentally-handicapped citizens take part in Special Olympics events all over the world to be selected to represent their country or state at the International Games. The goal of all competition is to help each athlete build a positive self-image, one that will carry over into the classroom, the home, the job, and ultimately, into a fulfilling life. It's impossible to put a price tag on smiles and the joy of satisfaction this competition brings.

My area of expertise is tennis for the handicapped. In cooperation with the United States Tennis Association, tennis programs for the disabled have been developed to bring the game to all individuals. When I first started to work with handicapped children in 1972, I experienced emotions difficult to define or explain. From them has evolved an important purpose in my life—to be a part of the development of sports and handicapped individuals.

In recent years there has been an influx of athletes with both mental and physical disabilities onto the tennis courts. Many organizations have contributed greatly to the development of the handicapped athlete. The United States Tennis Association (USTA) is proud to be at the forefront of these developments. As the national governing body of tennis, the USTA is committed to bringing the game to all populations. By working with the existing agencies for the disabled, the USTA is endeavoring to serve the emotional and athletic needs of all disabled athletes expressing an interest in tennis. A driving proponent in developing a tennis program for the clients was the Kansas

Association of Retarded Citizens. No one imagined that in just a few years there would be a state-wide tennis tour with over twenty tournaments and 1,500 participants. Thanks to the United States Tennis Association, in conjunction with the International Special Olympics, they have developed a seven-step skill test which measures the proficiency of each athlete as a preparation for match play at the games. Individuals who consistently achieved high scores were allowed to compete in supervised match play.

My first experience as a Director of Tennis on the Olympic level occurred in the summer of 1986 when the State Games were held at the University of Notre Dame at South Bend, Indiana. The planning and hours spent organizing and implementing the sport seemed both difficult and, at times, frustrating. But the day the event came, every minute of every day spent on the planning and preparation was well worth it. The volunteers involved were truly involved for the love of the sport and the athletes.

I'll never forget the wonderful expressions of accomplishment and joy on the faces of the athletes and the volunteers. Patience, love, and a need to be involved with the improvement of athletics at all levels are the only qualifications a volunteer needs to make a positive impact on the Special Olympics. The potential of Special Olympians is inspiring. They succeed because of their desire, determination, and support from family, friends, organizations, and volunteers who truly believe in sport in the purest form.

Notre Dame, Indiana

NOTES

1. Resources Used for Informational Purposes:

   United States Tennis Association
   Center for Education and Recreational Tennis
   729 Alexander Road
   Princeton, N.J. 08540

   Eunice Kennedy Shriver/Special Olympics, Inc.
   1350 New York Avenue N.W. #500
   Washington, D.C. 20005

THE NOTRE DAME VICTORY MARCH

Chorus:

Cheer, cheer for Old Notre Dame
Wake up the echoes cheering her name,
Send the volley cheer on high,
Shake down the thunder from the sky,
What tho the odds be great or small
Old Notre Dame will win over all,
While her loyal sons are marching
Onward to Victory.

THOUGH THE ODDS BE GREAT: THE SPIRIT OF NOTRE DAME

by Edward W. "Moose" Krause

In my forty-five years as player, coach, and Director of Athletics at the University of Notre Dame, I have often been called upon to speak about the "special spirit of the place." Some call it a winning spirit, a fighting spirit, the spirit of Rockne, Leahy, and Parseghian, or a spirit of excellence. The reality, I think, is a combination of the above. In the context of my experience of that "special spirit" at Notre Dame, I intend, in this short essay, to say again what I have often said before on the value of athletic participation and competition. Many kinds of lessons are commonly learned on the playing field. What follows is but a sampling of some of the more important ones. The reader should be assured that though sports became my lifework, a much lesser degree of involvement in the games will not deprive one of the benefits to be gained and of which I speak. Only later in life did it become clear to me that my experience in athletics at Notre Dame related to what classical Greek, Roman, and Christian culture would call a necessary training of the man in physical and moral virtue, especially the four cardinal virtues of the moral life, integrity, justice, self-discipline, and courage. Christian philosophers and theologians would also insist on the critical importance of developing one's faith and one's capacity for self-sacrificing love.

I grew up in "Back of the Yards" Chicago, of immigrant Lithuanian parents. I would never have had the chance for a college education except for the fact that my old high school football coach, Norm Barry, a teammate of the "Gipper," took me to see Notre Dame's renowned football coach, Knute Rockne. Rockne gave me an athletic scholarship. I owed my education to Rockne a second time when, during my freshman year, he intervened to keep me in school after I had been expelled by the Dean of the Science department. I had gotten a grade of 30 on a biology test because the corrector had made a mistake. It should have been 78. When the Dean wouldn't even look at my paper, I grabbed him by the coat in a peak of anger and was told to be off campus in "two hours." I went to Rockne to say goodbye, and I'll never forget the rather stern lecture he gave me on the importance of managing one's emotions. It was the first of many lessons. Because of the original corrector's error, Rockne saw to it that I got a second chance. I survived the incident to graduate eventually, with honors in English and Journalism, but I've always known that I was indebted to Coach Rockne not only for my education at Notre Dame--and that twice over--but, more importantly, for what became known as my "even disposition" and a host of other lifelong habits and attitudes.

Coach Rockne had remarkable success at Notre Dame. The "Fighting Irish" first gained national attention when, as a player, he teamed up with Gus Dorais to upset the great 1913 Army team, 35-13. That victory revolutionized college football, establishing the forward pass as a legitimate offensive weapon in the game. Dorais became Notre Dame's first All-American, and since then over 147 Irish players, including myself, have been similarly honored. Rockne became head coach at Notre Dame in 1918. A year later his team finished 9-0 and was named National Champion. In 13 years of coaching, his teams won 105 games, lost just 12, and tied 5, for an .897 winning percentage. In all he won six National titles and put together five unbeaten and untied teams. Later, his success would be rivaled, but never quite equaled, by Coaches Frank Leahy and Ara Parseghian. Leahy, in his time, posted an 87-11-9 winning record, including a four year post-war stretch when Notre Dame never lost a game. He won the National Championship four times. Parseghian won two National Championships in ten years, posting a 95-17-4 record.[1]

Others of us would attempt to carry on the Rockne tradition, even though our winning percentages would fall considerably below that of the master. I like to kid about the fact that I filled in as head football coach twice when Leahy was sick and won both games for a winning percentage of 100%. When pressed, I have to admit that my winning percentage as head basketball coach through eight seasons fell far below that. In fact, rather early on in my tenure as Athletic Director, I very wisely decided to "fire myself" as basketball coach and bring in Johnny Jordan from Loyola University. Winning, of course, is the goal of every coach and team, and the "will to win" is surely an important part of the Notre Dame Spirit, but there's a great deal more at stake than simply winning games in the special spirit of Notre Dame as I've come to know and cherish it.

At Notre Dame the athletic programs have always been clearly and very deliberately part of a larger educational effort. The University is justly proud of the fact that 97% of its student athletes graduate. Its players have won more academic scholarship awards than those at any other school in the country. I don't hesitate to say that in their day and in their own ways, Rockne, Leahy, and Parseghian were among the pre-eminent "professors" on our campus, not only in their effectiveness as teachers and leaders, but also in what they taught, and in the number and variety of people they were able to influence. It is very clear to me that Rockne taught more than the game of football. He taught a philosophy of life, a way of looking at life, and a way of living its opportunities, misfortunes, and challenges. He had once taught science as a protege of Fr. Julius Niewland, one of the many outstanding professors on campus. Later he chose to give up the classroom, but he never gave up being the teacher. He wanted to be a builder of men, and of character. He succeeded handsomely! As Notre Dame men, many of us would instinctively live out "the game and combat of life" in the same way we had played the game of football. The University's President, Father Theodore M. Hesburgh, after Ara's successful 1966 season, would put the point in these terms:

A football season is a lot like life in microcosm. The season begins with warm and sunny days filled with optimism and hope. As the season progresses, the sunshine wanes, the warmth diminishes, and optimistic hope is qualified by the hard lifelike realities of fierce competition, unexpected injuries, and the innate difficulty of sustained human effort. The days grow colder, the rains come, and optimistic vision becomes more realistic. It is always easier to declare the top position in anything than to reach it. While hope perdures, ultimate victory is again a fickle lady, ever to be wooed with all one's might, but never in this life to be securely or forever won. Each week is a new encounter; each season a new challenge. Life is like that too, because it is spent in time, amid all the vicissitudes of personal trials and existential difficulties...Kept within proper bounds of time, place, and emphasis, I believe strongly that the football season is indeed worthwhile...especially in the human qualities and habits it engenders in players and in those who follow the game--qualities of the spirit much larger and more important than the passing events that occasion them.[2]

Rockne and coaches like him taught a host of important lessons. They imbued their players with distinctive qualities of mind and heart that would become habitual and last a lifetime. First and foremost they taught us a basic honesty and integrity as we would seek to discover, to test, and to develop the talents and capacities God had given us. I mean here, first and foremost, that kind of honesty associated with self knowledge, with measuring and living within one's limitations, with identifying and capitalizing on one's strengths. This is clearly related to honesty and authenticity before others, fellow team members and fans as well as opponents. It was taken for granted that one of the limits to be respected were the written rules of the game and stated policies of the University. In my 45 years at Notre Dame there was never even a hint of impropriety or broken rules. Rockne and those who followed in his footsteps strove always to be an honest embodiment of the virtues they preached. He himself set the example of integrity, honesty, and respect for the rules.

Rockne was a master of the game in its technical and strategic side, but it was his understanding of its mental and emotional component that made him outstanding. I remember him insisting often that football was a game of wit and intelligence as much as it was of brawn and muscle. He taught his players how to concentrate on one thing at a time, on one play at a time, one day at a time. He would have us learn from, but not fret over, previous mistakes, fumbles, or missed plays. Nor would we muse distractingly over some future glory or score, but, rather, play the next point, as if it were the only one that counted. In a real sense it was, for it was the only one we could do anything about. And this was all part of a larger lesson. Anyone who plays a sport with intensity knows how important timing is, pacing oneself, and bringing the pieces and parts together to "peak" at the right moment. Just as timing and proper balance is a critical part of any game, so it is of life. A ball overthrown is just as useless as one underthrown. A shot hit too hard is as useless as one hit too soft. Too much studying or work would be just as harmful as too much playing, too much eating, or no praying. On the practice field we developed and learned many necessary physical skills, good blocking technique, good tackling, etc., but we were also schooled in numerous habits of mind and heart necessary for success in any sustained and serious human effort. Gradually, over a period of time and almost without our knowing it, we would come to acquire that keen practical judgment so necessary to the split-second timing and execution which is so much a part of athletic competition.

Another of the major lessons learned on the practice field would surely have to be what coaches commonly call teamwork. You come to realize the importance of coordinated effort, and how much as teammates you depend on one another. Some would learn leadership skills, others the importance of loyalty, but all of us a sharp sense of what we rightly owed to others. Success would necessarily be a shared endeavor and achievement. No one offensive player can execute a play, and no one defensive player can cover the entire field. There is a necessary harmony between a runner and his blocker, between a quarterback and his receiver, as each shifts his angles so as to trap defenders in futile movements. Every member of the team has a specific job to do, and one member's success or achievement depends on and inspires that of the others. I'll never forget how, on one occasion, when it seemed to Rockne that his famed "Four Horsemen" backfield might have been letting all the favorable publicity they were getting go to their heads, he deliberately played his second and third string linemen for over a quarter of one game to help bring home to that backfield how much they owed to their unsung teammates on the line. The famed "Four Horsemen" were stopped dead in their tracks until that first string line returned to the game. At halftime Rockne called for a vote: "Who was really more important, the line or the backfield?" The line won 7 to 4, and the coach had taught a lesson his players wouldn't soon forget.

None of the "Four Horsemen," by the way, weighed more than 163 pounds, and it was commonly acknowledged that as individuals they might not rank as "all time best," but as a unit they had no equal, and what they lacked in poundage, they more than made up for in speed, spirit, intelligence, and teamwork. Along with respect for our fellow teammates, Rockne would school us in respect for our opponents. He was grateful for the discipline which stiff competition would impose. He believed that a great team suffered if it was not sufficiently tested or challenged. As a result, Notre Dame would consistently seek to schedule and play the best. It was, Rockne maintained, no disgrace to lose to the best, but a real embarrassment for a good team to be beaten by an outclassed and weak opponent.

A third major cluster of virtues learned on the playing field would surely have to do with the importance of discipline and hard work. We became alert to the "cost of success," the kind of self-control and self-sacrifice entailed in the pursuit of any serious goal. At Notre Dame Coach Leahy , more than any other, epitomized the disciplinarian in pursuit of excellence. His practice sessions were so demanding that players commonly thought of Saturday, the "game day," as their "day off," their day to have fun. They would recount numerous anecdotes. One one occasion, when Johnny Lattner fumbled five times against Michigan State, Leahy ordered a football taped to Lattner's right hand for a week. He ate and slept with it, but never complained. All he ever said was, "I didn't fumble anymore after that, and I ended up winning the Heisman Trophy. Coach Leahy did what he had to, to make me the best I could be." On another occasion, in the course of a game with Pittsburgh, the offensive unit failed to make a first down after four tries, with only one yard to go. Even though Notre Dame won the game, Leahy ordered the team to a special practice session the following Sunday morning. They spent three hours practicing one yard plunges. He worried that that particular weakness could easily have cost us the game, and that team never again missed a first down on fourth and one.

In 1943, when Joe Sigliago broke his nose in a game, he ran to the sidelines suggesting that Coach Leahy might want to take him out of the lineup. The master took a long look at his nose and then barked in a rasping voice, "Well, it's broken now, you can't break it again. Get back in there and win this game for us!" Indeed, sports have no rival for training in self-discipline, perseverance, in the acceptance of adversity, and of the hard knocks of fate. Opportunities come in their own time and the individual can control neither their advent nor their frequency. Only in preparing oneself laboriously, steadily, through long hours of concentration, heat, weariness, and frustration, can one hope to be ready to take advantage of the opportunities that do come. In the midst of it all, one gains, I think, a positive sense of what human involvement in the real world with all its fateful ambiguity and many harsh limits normally entails.

Lastly, I should not fail to speak of that quality of courage and fortitude that the game of football in particular so obviously engenders and requires. It takes an unusual hardiness and stamina to challenge the fates, to risk everything in open competition, to face again and again the specter of defeat and public embarrassment until it no longer paralyzes you. In any single season or game there are many moments that try or test even the strongest or best of us. There are risky elements in the game, and many elements of pure luck or chance. But in this, too, the game simply mimics life. Sports exemplify, in numerous ways, the strategies, the tactics, the crushing disappointments, and the explosive "scores" that constitute our daily and working lives. They test, somehow, one's entire posture toward life, and in the testing even "losers" can win.

Gerry Faust lost more games than any other Notre Dame football coach, but in his own way, and in the only way he could, he was true to the Notre Dame spirit. He challenged the fates and strove mightily. He gave all that he could, and when that wasn't enough, he stepped aside with dignity and grace. In the worst of circumstances, when hounded and harassed by some of the press and dissatisfied alumni, he remained a gentleman and in control of himself, demonstrating again that we can not only survive the trials and tests that come our way, but in some respects even thrive in their midst. In what really counts, he was far from broken--integrity, fairness, self-control, fortitude and stamina. I have yet to meet a Notre Dame man who wasn't justly proud of him. This was reflected in the fact that, after five losing seasons, the graduating seniors of the class of 1986, in a gesture of respect, would call him back to the campus and honor him as "Senior Class Fellow."

Throughout virtually every season of play, as during most lifetimes or careers, one must expect to lose--and this despite one's best effort. To suffer defeat with grace and then to recover or bounce back is excellent preparation for life. Notre Dame players over the years have enriched our tradition with many great comeback victories and seasons.[3] It is the memory of those golden moments that have inspired and sustained many an alumnus and subway alumnus when, in real life, the "going got tough." We knew from our playing days that the last thing a Notre Dame man would do is quit or give up. What, one may ask, is the source of the power behind that relentless spirit?

Beyond the basic areas touching on integrity, teamwork, self-discipline, and courage, I would not be true to Coach Rockne and the spirit he did so much to engender at Notre Dame if I did not delve deeper to the bedrock foundation for his remarkable perseverance and the success it made possible. Father Charles L. O'Donnell, former President of Notre Dame, summed up the secret of Rockne's influence in the funeral oration he gave in 1931, after his tragic and sudden death in a plane crash in a Kansas wheatfield. Fr. O'Donnell concluded:

> In an age that has stamped itself as the era of the "go-getter"--all too often a ruthless thing-- he was a "go-giver." He made use of all the proper machinery and methods of modernity to be essentially not modern at all, but quite elementarily human and Christian, giving himself, spending himself, like water, not for himself, but for others. And once again in his life most illustriously is verified the Christian paradox--he has cast away to keep, he has spent his life to gain it.[4]

As Father points out, the ultimate source of Rockne's unique energy and capacity was his faith. In the tough, highly competitive arena of American collegiate athletics, I can say without embarrassment and without hesitation, what may surprise some, that, at its base, the special spirit of Notre Dame is religious. It is firmly and deeply rooted in the spirit of the

Gospels, in the life and work of Jesus Christ, in what He taught and in the kind of teacher He was. I say this as one deeply imbued with that spirit and charged for long years with carrying on its traditions. Historically, of course, Notre Dame and schools like it were founded and conducted over many years by men and women of deep faith. On the top of the University Church and in every room of the school, at the heart of the Gospels, is the cross, the suffering, death, and Resurrection of Jesus. The cross represents first and foremost a mystery of self-sacrifice, of radical love, and service. It is a witness to, and revelation of, God's love for us, but also stands for the care and concern it can inspire in our hearts for one another.

Enemies of faith deliberately misconstrue the matter. We don't reverence sacrifice or discipline pure and simple whether ours or that of Christ. As persons of faith and as Christian teachers we seek truth, we seek what is right or just, we seek to be faithful to our promises, and to those who belong to us, or we seek, as in Rockne's case, excellence on the playing field, but radically so, as Jesus does. Hence, we are ready, as Jesus was, to suffer if necessary in pursuit of fundamental goals, so serious is our commitment to them. To put the matter in slightly different terms, what the cross means is that because of who God is and what He has done for us, we don't give up; and because we don't give up, we don't fail. This faith of ours is a source of unique power, energy, and dedication if we let it permeate and direct our lives. We don't let the pettiness of others undermine our will to be generous. We don't let the anger of others undermine our will to bring about respect and reconciliation. We don't let the cynicism of others undermine our will to trust and believe in others. We can't let the failures and evils of a fallen world corrupt or destroy our will to do our best, and to do what is right. Our obedience to the God who made us, and who in Christ moves closer to us than we are to ourselves, must triumph over all who would undermine, corrupt, or destroy us.

It is our faith which allows us to face even death with a measure of confidence, and so, it goes without saying, every lesser evil on earth. Later in life I have had to endure many adversities. The heaviest was when my wife was paralyzed in an automobile accident. For four months she lay close to death. Now, after partial recovery and years of confinement in a nursing home, we carry on together, but it has been a veritable crucifixion for both of us. Prayer, our faith, and many other things have helped us through the trial, among which I would count my experiences on the playing field. The religious faith planted and nourished in those earlier years continues to energize all that we do together. In myriad and mysterious ways, we were told, it will reinforce, rescue, and redeem our integrity, our will to fairness, our will to self-discipline, and our courage, when these might otherwise fail or falter in a fallen and often violent world. Our faith allows us to give of ourselves to the bitter end, till death, and this--we can see it happening all around us--prepares us for a Resurrection. St. Paul, who obviously enjoyed games, since he refers to them so often in his epistles, put it this way:

> If we live as Jesus did, if we suffer and die as He did, i.e., if we are ready to sacrifice when necessary for the sake of what is true, and even to the point of death, if that kind of obedience and generosity characterize our lives, then we can be sure that we shall share as well the glories and joys of his Resurrection.[5]

Anyone who has deeply lived the Notre Dame spirit and mystique instinctively thinks beyond the Saturday football victories to the larger, much more serious Easter victory of Jesus and our call to share its mysteries when he hears the words of the school song, "The Notre Dame Victory March." Even when we lose, as will often be the case in the real world, as Jesus surely does on the cross, still we are confident of a deeper, more serious victory, if we have followed the way of the Lord, a victory over all that corrupts or weakens us, a victory over all that compromises and complicates our efforts. Because of our faith in God, and His promise to be with us, to sustain us, and finally to rescue us from the evils that afflict us, we never give up. And because we never give up, "what though the odds be great or small," Ole Notre Dame and her loyal sons and daughters will go on marching, marching onward to victory, the final victory, the only victory that really counts. That victory is a spiritual one over all that would defeat or demean us. This finally is the source of that luminous gleam in the Golden Dome. This is what people perceive and are

72

attracted to. The flashes of "excellence" on the playing field, as in other areas of life, are generated by and reflect the overwhelming power, beauty, and richness of the Christian gospel. And these are just a few of the lessons I first learned on the practice field from my old football coach. Of all the lessons I learned in college, they have proved to be among the most precious.

Notre Dame, Indiana

NOTES

1. Reliable and accessible sources on this tradition and its history include Dave Condon, Bob Best, and Chet Grant, Notre Dame Football: The Golden Tradition. South Bend: The Icarus Press, 1982; Ken Rapaport, Wake Up The Echoes: Notre Dame Football. Huntsville: The Strode Publishers, 1975; Francis Wallace, Notre Dame From Rockne to Parseghian. New York: David McKay Co., Inc., 1966; Chet Grant, Before Rockne at Notre Dame. South Bend: The Icarus Press, 1978; Fred Katz, The Glory of Notre Dame. London: Bartholomew House, Ltd., 1971; Ara Parseghian and Ton Pagna, Parseghian and Notre Dame Football. New York: Doubleday and Co., Inc., 1973; and many other similar sources.

2. The Rev. Theodore M. Hesburgh, "The True Meaning of the Game," Sports Illustrated, December 12, 1966, pp. 56-57.

3. See, for example, Jeff Jeffers, The 12 Greatest Notre Dame Football Comebacks. South Bend: The Icarus Press, 1981; or Mike Shields, Fight to Win: Great Moments in Notre Dame Football History. Chicago: Shillelagh Books, Inc., 1982.

4. The Rev. Charles L. O'Donnell, "The Everlasting Arms," Notre Dame Religious Bulletin. July, 1931, p. 1.

5. A paraphrase of I Corinthians 15. See also I Corinthians 9: 24-27, and II Timothy 4: 6-8.

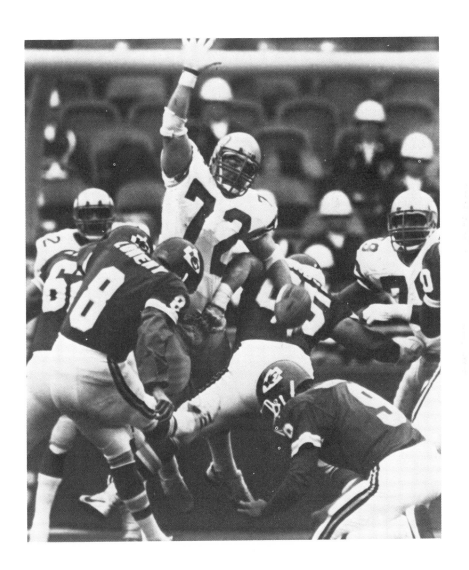

THE ROAD TO PROFESSIONAL SPORTS

by John W. Molloy, Jr.

Millions of young Americans play football each year. Thousands of young Americans play ice hockey each year. As they grow older the numbers get smaller. First, in junior high, the coach has to make cuts. Then in high school, even fewer play; some don't because they choose to concentrate on their studies, others because their classmates are better athletes. Then, the numbers dwindle even more in college. A fortunate few out of high school are good enough to earn a four-year scholarship because of their athletic ability. Finally, after college, the number that actually play professionally is minuscule when compared to all the ten-year-olds that start out playing the sport. However, our professional athletes are possibly held in such high esteem in the American public eye because there are so many people in our society today who remember playing in their youth.

Two athletes from Eastern Massachusetts, growing up less than forty-five minutes apart, have reached the pinnacle--professional sports. Michael O'Connell, born in Chicago but raised in Cohasset, Massachusetts, entered his twelfth season of playing professional hockey in the fall of 1986. Joe Nash, a native of West Roxbury, Massachusetts, entered his fifth season of playing on the defensive line in professional football in the fall of 1986.

O'Connell, known as a consistent and steady defenseman, has also achieved several prestigious milestones in his playing career. In the 1984-1985 season, O'Connell played in his 500th National Hockey League game, recorded his 200th NHL assist and registered his 300th career point. These milestones are significant because Mike is a defenseman whose goal is to stop the other team from scoring, yet he contributes significantly to his team's offensive attack, which is rare for a defenseman.

Mike had the opportunity in his career to play for his hometown team. In 1981 he was traded from the Chicago Black Hawks to the Boston Bruins. He played for the Bruins for six seasons. In 1986 he was traded to the Detroit Red Wings. Mike still holds the record for the longest goal streak by a Bruin defenseman with a seven game stretch in the 1983-1984 season.

Since the odds are very high against anyone reaching professional status in sports, it is interesting to take a look at the early careers of both O'Connell and Nash and see how each made his way from the sandlots and ponds of Massachusetts to professional sports. The author spoke to each of them in order to get a true perspective of the dedication, hard work, and hurdles that await an athlete on his way to the professional ranks.

Mike O'Connell played two years of hockey at Archbishop Williams High School. He thought that playing high school hockey would be a good stepping stone in the development of his hockey skills: "While I was playing at Archbishop Williams, I got a chance to play in the Boston Garden and realized that I did have a good chance at continuing to progress and play pro."

In his junior year of high school, he decided to play for a team called the Braintree Hawks in the New England Hockey League. Competing against such Massachusetts teams as Fitchburg, Lowell, Framingham, and such New Hampshire teams as Concord and Manchester, his team ended up winning the League title. Then the League folded. It was decision time for Mike O'Connell at a young age.

"I thought that everything was going in a positive way," explained the personable O'Connell:

> I had played two years of high school hockey, one year with the Braintree Hawks and I figured, well, now what am I going to do? I can't regress and go back to high school and play there, I don't think that I would have continued to develop. So I made the decision then, in my senior year in high school, to go up to Canada and play.

He played junior hockey at Kingston, Ontario, on the recommendation of Boston Bruins general manager, Harry Sinden.

At the time, there were only three or four Americans in the whole National Hockey League. The quickest, if not the easiest, way for a young American to break into the National Hockey League was to go to Canada and play junior hockey. Now there are many more Americans in the game. American college hockey programs have progressed so far in the past decade that they are now used as a major supplier of talent to the NHL.

After playing two seasons with the Kingston Canadiens, O'Connell was drafted by the Chicago Black Hawks as their third choice, 43rd overall in the 1975 amateur draft. He was also drafted by the Hartford Whalers of the NHL's rival league at the time, the now defunct World Hockey Association. Decision time, again? Not quite: "I knew that I would go right then [to the NHL]. I thought, I was 19 years old and I was ready to get on. I had two years away from home, and I was ready to continue to develop as a hockey player and also as a person."

His first two seasons as a professional were spent with Dallas in the Central Hockey League. In his second year with Chicago's top farm team, he was voted the Central Hockey League's best defenseman in the 1976-1977 season. That year he scored 15 goals and 53 assists for a total of 68 points, the highest point total in his career. O'Connell said:

I had three good years down there. They still didn't want to give me a chance up in the National Hockey League in Chicago. I could never understand that; they didn't have that great a team, but I guess they just decided that I might have been a little small (5'9", 185 lbs.).

Mike played six games with the Chicago Black Hawks in the 1977-1978 season, scoring a goal and an assist. The next season, O'Connell was called up from New Brunswick of the AHL in the fall.

79

They called me up on emergency recall; one of the defensemen got hurt, so I could stay up there as long as he was injured, but then he came back and they sent me back down. Bob Pulford (Chicago coach) said 'Mike, you're going to be right back up at the start of the year.' Being in hockey for as long as I'd been, when someone says that, you usually think, yeah, right, sure I will. But he stuck to his word and he gave me the chance, brought me up in January, and I've been up every since.

Three years of playing ice hockey in Dallas was a special experience:

Well, we didn't get too many people out to the games, except when we played Forth Worth. There was a small core of fans who followed the game, liked it, and understood it. There was a little bit of a different lingo in the game though. The boards were called the walls, and when there was a check made in the game, they called it a tackle.

In Dallas, Mike played for the only minor league team in Dallas. Dallas has the Cowboys (National Football League), Rangers (American League baseball), and the Tornado (professional soccer). So it was tough to get media coverage in the Dallas area.

"The media was fine," said O'Connell. "We had a writer; I think he was from the Minnesota area, and he did a great job. We got, not front page coverage, but we got second page coverage, and for the big win, they'd increase that coverage."

The media in the NHL is a lot different because of the fact that it is the NHL and most of the teams play in America's largest cities. O'Connell had this to say about it:

In the NHL, in some cities there is more coverage than in others. In Boston, there might be five newspapers and ten radio stations after the game. When we go to Canada, there might be ten newspapers and fifteen radio stations and there's usually TV people there every night getting interviews. Los Angeles--there's not quite as much coverage there as in Philadelphia; it's pretty much the same everywhere you go.

For the fan, the only way to get information about the team is through the radio, TV, or newspapers. The media plays an important part in professional sports. In 1986 Boston was privileged to have the New England Patriots go to the Super Bowl, the Boston Celtics win the NBA title, and the Boston Red Sox go to the World Series. Those three teams dominated the media coverage. Left to fight and scratch for space were the Boston Bruins. The Bruins had a successful season, making the playoffs before bowing out to the Montreal Canadiens in the first round.

When the Boston Bruins had Bobby Orr, considered by many the greatest player ever to play the game of ice hockey, the Bruins owned the city of Boston in his playing days, from 1966-1976. When he retired, the Celtics had a player named Larry Bird, who many feel is the greatest ever to play the game of basketball, and thus did fan and media support swing from the Bruins to the Celtics.

Does the professional athlete worry about what is written about him? Some do; Mike O'Connell doesn't. "I realize that the media has to do one thing, sell papers. That's the way I look at it. In any paper you pick up, you're going to read favorable or unfavorable things. Usually, you're going to read unfavorable things, because that sells more papers."

In all professional sports, the newspapers assign one writer, a beat writer, to cover a team for an entire season, from the opening of practice to the end of the season. Oftentimes, beat writers will stay with a team for a number of years. These writers often form friendships with players that are essential to the writer's getting his job done.

O'Connell:

> Personally, I have great rapport with all writers. I respect them, as I'm sure they respect me. They're doing their job and I'm doing my job. I try to treat everybody the same way. The trainers are a big part

81

of it, the writers are a big part of it, the TV people are a big part of it, and it's all a package; what we're trying to sell is the game of hockey, and I feel that I have a responsibility to do that, and I think that the only way we can do that is through the media. I bend over backwards for them, because they've always been real nice to me.

In addition to playing the game, there is also a lot expected from these athletes who ply their trade in the public eye:

As I said, I have a responsibility to sell this game, and I'll do anything for the organization I'm playing for. There's so many negative things in this crazy game of sports. If there's a great hockey game and there's a couple of fights, all they're talking about is the fights; they don't talk about the great plays made. So anything I can do through the media and through the people who are directly related to the media to help create a better image of the game, I'll do.

Part of promoting the game is public appearances. "Public-relations appearances are part of the job, but sometimes it can be a burden," said O'Connell. "You don't mind doing these things, but sometimes the timing is terrible. You have no control of the timing," he said but quickly added, "you don't mind doing it, but it just takes away from your personal time and that's precious during the 80-game season."

After the game, there are always fans awaiting their heroes and it's the professional athlete's duty to remember that they are looked up to by the fans. "After the games, there are always fans who want autographs," said O'Connell. "You don't really get a chance to meet them, you just sign autographs. There is usually a group of 30 or so fans and if you stopped and struck up a personal conversation with every one of them, you'd never get out of there."

In the 1986-1987 hockey season, Mike was in his first full season with the Detroit Red Wings. "I'm like a rookie out here," he told the <u>Boston Globe</u>. "In Boston, I didn't know how long I'd play. But here, I'd say three to five more years is a possibility, a definite possibility. In Detroit, the ice surface is bigger and instead of getting one second to react, you might get two seconds. It's a big difference. Really, I've been traded twice now, and both times it's been the best thing ever to happen in my career."

While with the Bruins, O'Connell had three consecutive fifty-point seasons. He has averaged nearly fifty points per season in his seven full years in the NHL. In addition, O'Connell played for Team USA at the World Championship tournament in Prague in 1985. An American, playing a Canadian game, Mike O'Connell worked his way from the rinks of Eastern Massachusetts to the National Hockey League.

The road to the National Football League has always been through college, and it's easier for an American to break into the NFL than it was for an American to break into the NHL, as was the case with Mike O'Connell. Football is one of America's most popular sports, as TV ratings on Sunday afternoons and Monday nights during the football season will attest to.

Joe Nash entered Boston College High School in the fall of 1974 and began his scholastic career on the freshmen football team. Joe proved to be one of the top players, and his sophomore year he was a starting defensive tackle for the varsity. When he was a senior, he completed his four-year playing career as Boston College High finished the season unbeaten and won the Division II Eastern Massachusetts Super Bowl title. Joe was a tri-captain and played both offense and defense and was named All-Scholastic by both the Boston Globe and the Boston Herald.

During his senior year in high school, Joe decided on Boston College. "One of the reasons that I went to Boston College was that it was so close to where I'd grown up," said Nash. "It's only about ten minutes from my parents' house in West Roxbury. Another major factor was that it was one of the few 'big' schools that offered me a scholarship."

While Boston College has recently gone to bowl games, the only bowl game that Nash played in was in Japan. "The only bowl I went to was in 1982, my first year at Boston College, the Mirage Bowl. We were 0-10 and played Temple in Japan," said Nash.

At Boston College, Nash played under two different coaches and feels that coaching is a big part of the game at that level. "I think that coaching was the biggest factor in the turnaround at Boston College. My freshman year, Boston College had probably more talent than it's had, maybe up until they started going to the bowls," said Nash. "We had Fred Smerlas (Buffalo), Jimmy Rourke (Kansas City), and I could name about ten other guys who either played in the pros or else went to the USFL and at least got a tryout and a chance to make the team."

Despite an outstanding four-year career as a starter at Boston College, when the day of the NFL draft came, Nash did not receive the call that a pro team had drafted him. Prior to the draft, several pro teams had come to Boston College to time him in the 40-yard dash, the measuring standard in pro football, and talked to him a little bit to try to get a feel for the type of person he was.

"During the draft, I got a few phone calls by people just checking in, what they want to do is keep the lines open for what becomes free agency," explained Nash. "When, finally, the end of the draft came, there were probably four teams that wanted me to play for them, or at least showed some interest in me signing."

Then some teams started backing off just a little. They were still interested, but once they start signing other free agents, it becomes a numbers game. If a player like Nash doesn't sign early with a team, he ends up not signing with them at all.

How did he wind up with the Seattle Seahawks? "Seattle showed a lot of interest in me, besides, they play a four-man line, which gives them another extra lineman on the roster; and the fact that they offered me more money than anybody else did, that was the major factor," explained a smiling Nash.

As the world of professional sports has become more of a business than a game, all players are now represented in contract negotiations by an agent. It's interesting how that process works, how a pro football player decides which agent will represent him.

"Agents come to you," said Nash. "Mostly you go by word of mouth, how other people have felt about him. Now, I'm

represented by Sports Advisors Group, which is based in Boston."
He went on:

> The contract itself is a standard contract; everybody
> has the same basic contract. The problem that you
> get into is the amount of money that you want and
> how you want it paid out. Usually, the amount of money
> is set; they pay you this amount of money, then it's
> just a question of how you want to get paid, whether
> you want some of it up front or things like that.

In 1986, Joe entered his fifth season with the Seattle Seahawks.
He is one of only a few free agents who have made a career
in pro football. Not only that, but Nash made it to the Pro
Bowl, football's all-star game in 1984. In 1985, with 12 sacks,
Joe Nash was the second leading quarterback sacker of all
the nose tackles and was the fourth leading tackler on the
team. It was a long way from when Joe arrived at the Seattle
training camp in 1982.

"When I was a rookie, you used to have to get up and sing your
school song," Nash explained of rookie initiations. "That really
isn't that difficult to do, although some guys don't even know
their school songs," he said laughingly.

He explained that the guys who were a little cockier than
others got a little more hazing. There were guys that had
trash barrels full of water leaned up against their door, so
when they opened it in the morning, the water would spill
into their rooms. A couple of other guys had their rooms trashed
at night by the veterans, although Joe noted that it's mostly
in fun, nothing really serious. The Seahawks, however, no
longer have any rookie initiations.

When asked to give advice to Mike Ruth, a rookie nose tackle
with the New England Patriots in 1986, Nash told the Patriot
Ledger, "The only advice I have for him is to keep his head
on a swivel because you get hit from all sides in this league
when you're in the middle."

There are several other differences between college football
and pro football, "First of all, it's more of a business," said
Nash.

He said that a typical day in the season was not an easy 9-to-5 desk job. Sometimes, if he has to get treatment, his day will start at 7:30 a.m. If he wants to lift weights, then he's in at 9:00. He has meetings from 10:00 until it's time to go to practice. After a two to three hour practice, you might have to lift some more weights or have other duties, and you don't leave until five. Then after work, you have to bring film home and study the film.

"It's more of a business attitude in the pros," said Nash. "Plus the athletes, you've got a better group of athletes, you've got a pick of the 'crop,' everything's been trimmed down."

Nash has appeared in the Pro Bowl and explains that there are a lot of factors that go into player selection. It is based on more than just ability and the type of season an individual player is having.

> The won-loss record is certainly a big factor in post-season honors. If you make it to the playoffs, you've got a better shot at getting in than if you're a great player on a team that is not winning. You may be a better player, but what happens is, when your team is playing well and winning, you get more publicity, because that's how you win in football, by the big play.

While pro hockey is fighting a battle to be recognized nationally in the sports pages, there is no such problem with pro football, whose place in the media is solid.

"I get along well with most writers," said Nash, although he admits that there are certain days after practice that he just wants to slide past them and get back to the locker room. The Seahawks have days during the week where the locker room is open and reporters can come right into the locker room and talk with the players. However, on other days it is off limits.

Joe and his fellow Seahawks do care about what's written about them and take exception to unfair journalism. "We have a writer in Seattle that used to really put the Seahawks down," Nash explained slowly. "Nobody even knew who the guy was;

we don't even know if he ever came by." What frustrated Joe was that he was not able to know who the writer was, and that was what was upsetting.

"For the most part though, you get along great with the writers because usually they're there to help you," said Nash. He felt that most beat writers won't write too many bad things, unless there is something obvious. They do that because they have to keep the lines of communication open.

Joe stated a common opinion of football players: "If they (writers) start running around bad-mouthing players, players aren't going to want to talk to them." Thus there is a delicate balance in the relationships between pro players and sports writers.

Fortunately for Joe Nash and the Seattle Seahawks, no difficult situation has arisen, but if it should, the reaction of the Seahawks would probably include the blackballing of the writer.

So there it is, the story of two players, not high-priced draft picks earmarked for the Hall of Fame before they ever played a minute of pro ball. But two players who overcame the long odds against them and have gone on to become consistent performers for their teams, and who, most importantly, have given us much to admire.

Quincy, Massachusetts

87

SPORTS AND THE FAMILY

by Albert K. Wimmer and Linda Morgan

The singles championships at the 1986 U.S. Open Tennis Championships at Flushing Meadows, New York, were decided among four players, all from the same country, Czechoslovakia, and raised under similar circumstances. There is no question that the precious few who reach such heights in athletic competition are exceptional individuals who may be able to store hundreds of thousands of past experiences in their minds, make finely tuned gradations among them, and respond instantly to them with "gut feelings" (2).

A study by educational researchers at the University of Chicago found that it usually takes from ten to fifteen years for successful athletes to move from the relatively simple beginnings to the complex and difficult processes that make them experts in a field. Interestingly, the study also revealed that expertise may be something that many more people could reach, given the right nurturing and motivating conditions in the home (3: p. 1). There appears to be a generally acceptable proficiency formula which is based on the fact that past patterns and experiences are recognized and employed in given situations regardless of whether one is an experienced musician or athlete (2). For instance, the more talented the athlete, the more typical situations he or she will have stored than less-talented athletes. They have a "finer gradation of them and a better ability to see the similarities" (3: p. 3).

What interests us here is not really the process by which the beginner becomes an expert. Rather, it is the environment of nurturing and encouragement which is provided by the sports-oriented family that is of interest. This is not to minimize the role played by enthusiastic teaching which makes learning a challenging and joyous process (2).

Let us return briefly to the "Czech phenomenon." Among the top ten women players in the world there are three native

Czechs, and among the top 150 players among the men, there are seven, two among the top ten. Granted, Czechoslovakia maintains a special academy for talented tennis players. However, the fact remains that the top-ranked players are all products of tennis families, in some cases generations, such as Martina Navratilova whose grandmother once defeated Helena Sukova's grandmother in a Czech national tournament. Conversely, Ivan Lendl's father, Jiri, was once ranked 15th among Czech players, and his mother, Olga, was the second-ranked woman in the country at one time.

The following observations do not pretend to be a final word on the relationship between a nurturing family atmosphere and athletic success; rather, they are intended as an expose of sorts in which the authors relate their experiences as parents of athletes. The writers will use an approach which goes beyond the overt manifestations of athletic success, that is, awards and peer recognition. They are attempting to probe into the factors that figure decisively in the nurturing atmosphere mentioned above as well as an appraisal of how the family is in turn affected by the athletic success of some of its members. A two-pronged approach is intended; a look at athletics and the family as it is remembered by one of the authors and as it is experienced daily by the other. Thus, the essay will necessarily have to be in two parts.

Some researchers tend to stress the effect the family has on the athlete, thereby shelving the many benefits the family as a whole derives from the success of one of its members (2).

A Retrospective View of the Relationship Between Family and Sports

There are several categories of catalysts which all could be subsumed under the general heading of interaction and personal growth. Athletes in this country are not only more popular and more accepted by their peers, but they also benefit from the exposure they get to the parents and friends of other athletes, as well as the general public. Public recognition, however, not only follows the athlete, but also the members of his or her family. Many a parent has made friends while attending an athletic event. Indeed, even such personal matters as the choice of one's private physician may change, resulting in switching family doctors simply because personal interaction during athletic events may have led to a genuine relationship of trust and friendship. Car-pooling may have a similar effect on family members.

It is impossible to measure the benefits some family members derive from the fact that there are athletes in the family. If the parents are not already active in a given sport, the very fact that a child shows athletic promise may get the parents involved to the extent that the parent, too, profits through increased health and a feeling of well-being which then may set in motion a life-time attitude that will afford the parent long-term benefits long after the child has left the home.

The presence of an athlete in the family may lead to an altered lifestyle where a previously ignorant parent gains insight into the physiology of sports as well as a degree of nutritional awareness. Again, the effect of this can be rather long-term.

Competition carries with it the agony of defeat and the exhilaration of victory. It is the agony of defeat which does not just set on after the fact but is also responsible for most of the apprehension preceding athletic competition, which may have a rather negative effect on the psychological atmosphere in the family. Conversely, athletic competition, and certainly success, helps release tensions which otherwise could adversely affect communication and interaction within the family.

On the matter of discipline, both athlete and parent together learn to subordinate their lives to things other than daily routines, breadwinning, running a business, leisure time activities, family routines, and schoolwork, resulting in a new dimension of discipline with different demands on time, consideration, and common sense.

The athletic activities of children can have a profound effect on the parents. Their own "self-confidence" can grow with every success and shrink with every failure. Nurturing parents will be above such destructive behavior. They will neither exult nor belittle success; nor will they minimize or exaggerate failure. There exists an obvious danger for parents to become so wrapped up in the athletic fortunes of their children that they turn into tyrants of the worst sort, attempting to hold their children to the successes they never achieved themselves and reliving the frustrations they may have experienced in their own mediocre days. Therein lies a great danger. Not only can such behavior lead to alienation between parents and children, but to a self-esteem that is not rooted in the child itself, but depends on the parents' moods. Also, the previously mentioned bonus for parents which can be found in the fact that their circle of friends increases as their child participates more and more in athletic competition can turn into just the opposite when the unduly partial parent becomes offensive to the parents and friends of other competitors, boring them with the praises of their offspring and offending them with their blind partiality.

Experiencing Family Sports From Day to Day

The word "sport" is rooted in Latin and literally means "carry away" (1). "Sport," as defined by Webster's New World Dictionary, is "any activity or experience that gives enjoyment or recreation; pastime; diversion." It is thought that sports originated with the necessity of man to be victorious over his enemies as well as from an innate need of primitive man to play games, probably for the purpose of relaxation and easing of tensions. Considering the seriousness with which Americans (along with people in some other countries of the world) take their participation, and viewing of, sports, the building up of tension, rather than its release, is often more noticeable.

This is not to say there is not a definite physical release of tension after having participated in a sports event, but it seems the mental preparation and emotional letdown following the actual event are sometimes difficult to deal with. This can be trying not only for the actual sports participant, but for those who associate with the competitor, especially the immediate family. Parent observers of an athletic event have often been overheard to say "This is so much tougher on me than it is on my child." I have never yet seen a parent who has not exhibited some expression of either joy or despair, depending on the outcome of the sporting event.

Children in our society are taught from a very early age to be aggressive, competitive, and unswerving in their quest for victory. This often, unwittingly, starts when parents play games with children to see who can get dressed fastest or who can finish their dinner first. Many parents employ the tactic of game-playing with their children, primarily because it is easier to get a small child to cooperate in getting dressed, eating a certain food, etc., by making a competitive game of the situation rather than demanding blind obedience to a direct order. The game-playing is fun for the child and certainly less taxing for the parent, so we assume that everything works out for the best. There is the possibility this practice of game-playing might, at a very early age, begin to form that determined, aggressive, super competitive spirit which is needed to be an outstanding athlete.

Many children seem to have a personality which thrives on competition. They want to be involved in every sport that comes along, and they want to be the very best in each one. While parents want to be supportive, it's sometimes difficult to know just how much support is needed to give encouragement without applying undue pressure to succeed. Parents are sometimes caught in a rather precarious situation regarding this. Some children are never happy with their performance in a sports event, no matter how many times they are reassured by family and friends. Other children seem to feel quite pleased while their spectator parents may view their performance as somewhat inadequate. So what does a parent do or say in these situations without creating even more tension for the young athlete?

An important question to ask about the tension which is present in a sports-oriented family is whether or not this is a "healthy" tension. Children sometimes participate in sports completely on their own initiative, perhaps influenced by their peers. This is something they want to do and which they enjoy. Other children are "pushed" into sports by parents who may actually be the competitive ones and who enjoy participating vicariously through the efforts of their children. If the child really is not the aggressive, competitive type, the tension involved in sports participation may not be that healthy. The child may be participating in sports because he or she senses that it is the parents' wishes, and that child may feel a real inner conflict; however, if the child in question is definitely aggressive, competitive, and goal-oriented, sports may provide a very healthful tension which can be an outlet for the child's frustrations from other areas of life. In James A. Michener's book, Sports in America, he mentions the problem of adults who try to act out their sports dreams through their children:

> The evil always begins with adults who desperately want to win championships which were denied them when they were boys. They use children, often not their own, to achieve this dream, and in doing so, pervert the normal experiences of youth. With shocking frequency they destroy the child's interest in further sports, and the outcome of their overly ambitious programs is apt to be a cynical realization by the children that they have been misused (4: p. 117).

Michener also states "a sense of competition is natural in children, provides healthy emotional outlets and must not be suppressed; but it should not be exaggerated, either" (4: p. 119).

The family picture becomes even more complicated when there are two or more children in a family who are involved in sports. The obvious difficulties are the time scheduling and car-pooling which necessarily have to be taken into account for different practice times and perhaps different practice locations. Even though this appears to be a deterrent to family sports participation, it can actually be an incentive for families to develop a more organized and carefully planned lifestyle. It becomes increasingly complicated for parents to give equal time and support for each participant, and it may become necessary for parents to alternate attendance at children's sporting events. If the children are assured of their parents' emotional support, an occasional absence shouldn't have too great an impact on a child's performance or attitude.

Parents have to take into account the differences in the emotional and physical characteristics of their children and how those relate to a particular child's success, or lack of success, in athletic activities. One child may be as talented and skilled in a particular sport as an older sibling but yet be emotionally disinclined to give complete body and soul in an effort to be a top performer. Parents often see the potential in their child and are tempted to encourage them to work harder in order to succeed as an older brother or sister may have. This is an opportunity for the parents to exercise discipline and realize that being the "best" may not be as important to one child as it is to another. Parents must be willing to support and encourage the level of performance that child is prepared to give.

Still other children, for reasons of physical makeup, may not be as suited for certain sports as a brother or sister may have been. That child may realize this and choose not to participate in sports. On the other hand, he or she may work very hard in sports to attain success but never be able to reach quite the heights which a brother or sister reached. It's somewhat frustrating for both child and parents, but parental support and encouragement must be expressed for the effort put forth, and not necessarily the measured success of that effort. In the words of the great basketball star, Wilt Chamberlain, "The true spirit of sport is not how tall you stand nor how high you reach. It's how much you give of what you have to give."

Whether or not a child is considered "successful" in their sport does not affect some of the benefits gained from participation. The child is proud of the accomplishment of "making the team," and this pride carries over to the rest of the family. Earning a place on the team is a reward for hard work, and friends and family share in the sense of accomplishment which an athlete feels. Athletes are very much admired in our society because of the determination and hours of practice involved in becoming one of the "best." The young participant in sports develops self-discipline and the capacity to recover after a disappointment and continue working toward success.

All sports, irrespective of their origin, developed in man faculties that have enriched his life manifold. They trained him in endurance, hard work, and vigorous self-control, gave him stamina and the will to do his best, no matter what. Some of the greatest lessons of life have come out of the world of sport. They have taught man to be undaunted by any challenge. Athletics, from the Greek, embodies the 'prize' (athlon) awarded to the winning contestant. Yet, failing to gain it, the true sportsman also knows how to take defeat. He will always be ready to try again and strive to attain what has never before been achieved (1: p. 6).

The importance of sports in our lives is reflected in the use of such phrases as "playing the game," and "hitting below the belt," and referring to someone as being a "spoilsport." All of these expressions originate with our society's emphasis on sports. Sports events seem to foster a cooperative spirit with the spectators as well as the players. This is especially true on the family level. Everyone exults in the victories and shares in the grief of the defeats. It's an important learning and sharing experience for each family member.

Notre Dame, Indiana
Bristol, Indiana

BIBLIOGRAPHY

1. Brasch, R. How Did Sports Begin? New York: David McKay Co., Inc., 1970.

2. Dreyfus, Stuart, and Dreyfus, Hubert. Mind Over Machine. New York: Free Press, 1985.

3. Marinucci, Carla. "Perfection: Tracing Traits That Separate the Experts From the Novices," Chicago Tribuine, 1986, Sept. 4, Section 5, p. 1.

4. Michener, James A. Sports in America. New York: Fawcett, 1983.

SPORT IS ALIVE AND WELL IN RACQUETBALL DOUBLES

by Saul Ross

Human beings appear to have a penchant for defining and categorizing. These activities, which are similar in nature, have important psychological and educational implications since they enable us to move about in our world and help us to understand it.

In addition, as will be seen shortly, certain philosophical issues are raised whenever we become engaged in these endeavors in a formal way. Defining something and then fitting it into a neat "pigeonhole" helps us to grasp its meaning and also enables us to envisage many, if not most, of its attributes. Once we place something in its proper slot and name it, we then seem to "own" it. Since we generally attribute a number of qualities to everything in a given category, the importance of placing only similar things together is obvious.

Questioning the validity of each category is one of the tasks performed by philosophers who can approach the problem in a number of ways. Issues can be raised regarding the manner in which the category was determined or the procedure used in developing the definition. Sometimes the actual validity of the category or definition is questioned---are the differentiae sufficient to set the category clearly apart from all other similar and dissimilar objects? If they are not, then many other sorts of things become admissible, resulting in a classification that is much too broad, or all-encompassing, to be useful. Another way of dealing with this type of problem is to ask the most basic question---does the definition truly reflect what is, what actually exists? The second and third approaches just mentioned form the basis from which a challenge to conventional thinking about sport was mounted by the noted American philosopher, James Keating. He is one of the first contemporary philosophers to study sport, and his scholarly efforts have produced many interesting and important insights. As a result of some of his analytic efforts, certain conclusions emerged which need further consideration in light of three factors: my own experience in racquetball doubles, an analysis of that experience in light of Keating's arguments, and the presence of a certain theory in one of the most exact of the sciences, physics.

I. "Sport" Does Not Exist

In a series of articles published between 1963 and 1965, Keating (3: p. 105) insisted upon a rigid dichotomy between the terms "sport" and "athletics." He confesses that his own efforts in this regard might have contributed to the confusion instead of helping to clarify matters. As his thinking on this issue evolved, Keating (3: p. 104) became "convinced that the word 'sport' is so hopelessly ambiguous that its careless and promiscuous use precludes any meaningful discussion and communication." Sport, as a word which defines a set of activities and describes a category of human behavior, fails in its task in Keating's opinion and, due to its ambiguity, it does not truly reflect what actually exists. The basis for Keating's conclusion is his detection of two distinct, and radically different, activities encompassed within that one definition/category we usually refer to as sport. Two such diverse, and incompatible, activities cannot be accommodated when subsumed under a single definition or in one category.

What are these two distinct, diverse, incompatible activities? And what makes them so different that they cannot be accommodated within one definition or in one category? A description of both categories helps provide the answer. One set of activities is characterized by Keating (3: p. 105) as highly competitive in which the goal of the competitors is honorable victory in the contest. Such activities fit under the heading "athletics," a term deemed appropriate for etymological and historical reasons. Striving to win, in compliance with the rules, in physical contests designed to determine excellence through honorable victory in a contest, is the distinguishing feature of athletics. Play, in sharp contrast, "is a free creative activity in which the goal of the participants is to maximize the joy of the moment, seeking no goal outside the activity itself" (3: p. 110). Among the evidence Keating offers in support of his two-category (athletics-play) proposal is an invitation to engage in introspection, to examine one's own experience and motivation. This process, he believes, will lead to agreement with his basic view: sport, as a term and category, cannot encompass such diverse activities as those which are subsumed under athletics and play. The activities we engage in are either athletics or play but not, according to Keating, sport.

II. A Re-examination of the Situation

There is obvious merit in attempting to distinguish between athletics and play, as Keating suggests, but there are some activities which just do not fit smoothly, if at all, into this dichotomy. Keating's analysis and conclusion appear to be based, in large part, on the attitude toward participation and the motives of the individual participant. An analysis of motives and attitudes is a difficult, challenging exercise which needs to be undertaken with great care. Without wishing to enter the realm of Freudian psychology, or engage in a debate about the validity of his theory, I want to make one basic claim that prevails under all schools of psychology: more often than not, there are a number of motives, intertwined and intermingled, rather than only one, involved in determining and explaining behavior. This assumption forms the basis of one line of counterargument against the proposal made by Keating.

To support his position, Keating invites his readers to engage in introspection. His invitation is accepted with one major qualification---the various comments made about racquetball doubles come as much from my friends who play with me as those which resulted from my own introspective efforts. The comments were made during the course of casual conversation over the years and are not formal replies to queries posed in a specially designed questionnaire. These expressions accurately reflect the feelings of the players since they were offered spontaneously in the free flow of the banter athletes engage in before, during, and after a game.

Basically, I shall argue that racquetball doubles, as played by the group which I am associated with, is an activity which has the features Keating attributes to athletics; yet, at the very same time, it also has the features he attributes to play.

A rebuttal to Keating's proposal emerges from an investigation of two areas. The first is the careful consideration given to the diverse, and at times seemingly contradictory but yet accurately valid, ways in which the activity and its attributes can be described. The second is a review of the motivation of the players. A logical extension of my rebuttal calls for a reassessment of the two seemingly mutually-exclusive categories, athletics and play.

III. Racquetball Doubles

Racquetball, a recent arrival on the scene, has enjoyed an unprecedented meteoric rise in popularity. It has attracted millions of players within a very short period of time. Many of the first players were converts from handball who chose to switch rather than fight the swelling tide of racquetballers usurping the handball courts. The facility I play at has two courts, originally designed for handball but now used almost exclusively for racquetball. My associates and I play racquetball at noon, and a certain protocol has evolved which guides play and also reflects our collective value system. In turn, this protocol serves to reinforce the inherent values embedded in it. Since time and space are at a premium at noon and the goal is to accommodate the maximum number of participants, doubles is given priority over singles. Games of singles and cut-throat are permitted only if no one is waiting. Where there are fewer than four racquetballers in the court, a player who arrives on the scene need only knock on the door to gain admittance. First come, first served is the rule which ensures maximum utilization of both courts.

Teams are organized based on an informal rating system which is aimed at equalizing competition. At the end of the game the winning team remains in the court and the losers leave. If only one person is waiting, a lottery system is used to determine which player on the losing team leaves and which one stays. With the introduction of one or two new players, the winning team may be split up with each player acquiring a new partner to ensure equality of competition for the next game. When three players are waiting, the lottery system applies to the winning team; one member of the winning team, along with the two from the losing side, are replaced. Under this protocol, everyone gets to play according to time of arrival and the rotation is governed by which team wins and which team loses.

Racquetball as Athletics - Once the teams have been determined and the game starts, the players compete vigorously, striving for an honorable victory in the contest. Adherence to the constitutive rules of the game is an integral part of the protocol. Racquetball doubles is a zero-sum game; one team's attainment of the goal, victory, precludes its achievement by the other team. As described above, racquetball doubles certainly fits under the heading, "athletics." This categorization would be confirmed by spectators watching the players move about the court to the best of their ability in their attempt to score enough points first to emerge victorious.

Athletics, as delineated by Keating, focuses on competition and winning, clearly implying that the major, and perhaps sole, consideration for entering the contest is striving to win, or actually enjoying the fruits of victory. Indeed, striving to win, in accordance with the rules, is the main differentia, the feature which distinguishes athletics from play. Spectators watching us play racquetball doubles would be justified in concluding that we are engaged in an athletic contest rather than being involved in play. However, before drawing that conclusion, other factors need to be considered.

Is striving to win the main motivating factor for these racquet-ballers? It is not, according to their comments. Striving to win is important; to do less than your best is to behave dishonest-ly toward your partner and, at the very same time, it insults the members of the other team since they are not challenged to operate at their highest level of skill. Striving to win, for us, is a motivator which we seem to need to induce us to con-tinue participating in vigorous physical activity. Taking a noon-hour calisthenics class, be it exercise or aerobics, is just too boring, a situation confirmed by declining attendance in all such programs. Striving to win is important for many valid reasons but for us, as a motivational factor, its prime utility is promoting continued participation.

A clear insight into this important clarification is offered by Simon (4: p. 15) who notes the need to "distinguish the conceptual claim that the goal of competition is victory from the psychological claim that the competitors' primary motive for participating is the desire to win." Competing has a certain excitement, a happy tension when kept in perspective, which many people relish; the process can be more important and edifying than the outcome. This prevails in our situation as confirmed by comments such as, "that was a terrific game, everyone had a really good workout," and "boy, that game was so close, every stroke counted." Statements such as these invariably come from both teams. Even though every effort was made to defeat the opponent, as it should be in an athletic contest, Simon's (4: p. 15) point is pertinent here: "it doesn't necessarily follow that the main reason they have for competing is to win." Other motivating factors---good health, weight reduction, weight control, friendship, stress management---may be equally, or even more, important. The discussion continues.

Winning within the rules is another feature of athletics. In racquetball doubles we adhere explicitly to the rules by calling our own faults and errors. An honor system is in force, one that works more effectively than in games where a referee is present. Full responsibility for ensuring that the rules are obeyed remains with the players rather than being delegated to another party, the referee or umpire. As we play racquetball the "game-within-a-game," attempting to outwit the referee, cannot exist. Every player takes full responsibility for making correct calls honestly, for without this commitment, and its full implementation, the game could not be played.

Striving to win an honorable victory in accordance with the rules is manifestly clear in the game of racquetball doubles we play. At times, particularly when the teams are well matched, the level of intensity is extremely high as each player scoots around the court executing the various offensive and defensive skills and maneuvers which constitute the game. We compete vigorously, but this needs to be understood in the following light:

Opponents are engaged in the cooperative enterprise of generating challenges against which they can test themselves. Each has the obligation to the other to try his or her best. Although one wins and the other loses, each gains by facing a test that each voluntarily chooses to undertake (4: p. 21).

Competition exists but so does cooperation since the team we play with are both our opponents and also our partners.

It appears that in many ways racquetball doubles can be subsumed under the heading "athletics," but for a number of valid reasons, it does not appear to fit.

Racquetball as Play - Play, as defined by Keating (3: p. 110), "is a free creative activity in which the goal of the participant is to maximize the joy of the moment, seeking no goal outside the activity itself." All of us who participate in racquetball doubles do so freely, on our own accord. We are not forced to play nor compelled to become involved. At times we check to determine if enough players will be present on a certain day, but that cannot be construed as coercion. We play simply because we want to and so, on that basis, racquetball doubles now appears to fit nicely under the heading of play.

Further support justifying this categorization emerges from the description of play as a creative activity. Constant creativity is the hallmark of all our games. Each time the ball is put into play the receiver needs to take all pertinent factors---score, position of partner and opponents, strengths and weaknesses of all, general strategy, specific tactics---into consideration in determining which shot to use. As each game evolves, new conditions emerge demanding creative responses from all the players. Each creative response appears to be additional evidence supporting the view that racquetball doubles is play, but yet, at the very same time these creative acts are part of the concerted effort exerted to win an athletic contest.

During play in racquetball doubles, joy is maximized often, just about every time one of us executes a kill shot, hits a fine passing shot, or makes a good return. Good shot-making is a source of joy, with the enjoyment increased by the compliments received after a good play from one's teammate and, as often, from one's opponents. Improvement in ability, as manifested in better play, is a continuing source of joy during the moment when it is being experienced. Placing the ball exactly where you want it, under the wide range of circumstances which prevail during the game, adds to the enjoyment derived and becomes a goal within the activity itself. However, as Thomas (5: p. 187) observes, focusing on the joy of the moment "does not necessarily mean that striving to win becomes unimportant." Each instance of good shot-making contributes simultaneously to two goals, maximization of joy and winning an honorable victory in an athletic contest.

Why do we continue to play racquetball? While each participant may cite a number of different reasons (health benefits, weight control, stress reduction, friendship), there is consensus on one point: we play for the joy of it. We enjoy playing and we derive joy from our participation. Joy comes from the play attributes of racquetball doubles and, in equal measure, joy comes from the athletic attributes of racquetball doubles. If asked directly, I doubt that any one of the players could separate the sources of joy, assigning a greater degree to one or the other. Both elements, play and athletics, are inexorably intertwined and integral to the way we play and view the game.

IV. A Proffered Resolution

Racquetball doubles, as we play it, can be subsumed under the heading of athletics, but such a listing would not be completely accurate. Conversely, racquetball doubles, as we play it, can be subsumed under the heading of play, but that too would not be a truly apt categorization. Racquetball doubles, as we play it, is a highly competitive game in which the goal of the competitors is honorable victory in the contest but, at the very same time, for us, it is a free creative activity where our goal is to squeeze all the joy out of the moment; we seek no goal outside the activity itself. One key to understanding this seemingly contradictory situation is to place competition and winning in perspective. For us, competition is important as the motivator which promotes participation and adds structure to the activity but it never becomes the overriding factor. Within that context, winning is what we strive for but victory becomes a secondary consideration, replaced in importance by the enjoyment of the game. However, it is also important to note that striving to win adds to the enjoyment we derive.

It may be surprising, and confounding for some, to accept the proposition that the same phenomenon can be described in two different, and seemingly incompatible, ways as I have just done. This situation is not confined to racquetball; such is also the case in the Wave-Particle Theory in physics where light is explained as follows:

One group of phenomena, comprising what is usually called classical optics, points to the wave nature of light, in accordance with the predictions of classical electromagnetic theory. Another class of phenomena, observed in more recent years, points with equal force to the particle nature of light (6: p. 220).

To exacerbate matters, it is now the accepted "belief that both matter and radiation have a dual character, emerging as wave-like in some situations and as particle-like in others" (1: p. 810, emphasis added). Viewing light and matter in terms of particles appears to be in direct conflict with the wave description but Young (6: p. 220) states, "the accepted viewpoint today is that they are not incompatible." A description is determined, in part, by the perspective taken. Hecht (2: p. 260) explains, "Light manifests itself as particle or wave, and which we 'see' depends on how we look." One perspective yields one description and another purview yields another conception.

Physics, one of the most exact of the sciences, has difficulty accounting for a basic, specific phenomena, light, in an unequivocal way. Human beings, by their very nature, are much more complicated, and human behavior is much more complex, due to factors such as intention, aspiration and motivation. We do not behave strictly in accordance with physical laws but rather innovate responses to constantly-changing environments. Explaining human behavior is much more intriguing and challenging; neat categories, into which we can place diverse activities, are far more difficult to devise. Sport, as a category, can be replaced by two other classifications, athletics and play, but to do so creates a void. My involvement with racquetball doubles has enabled me to use it as an experiential base for comments and insights. Many of the same comments can be made about a great number of games which we, as human beings, play. In such games, where the attributes of athletics and the attributes of play can be ascribed to the very same activity, the best name to give to the activity, in my opinion, is sport.

Ottawa, Ontario

The research assistance of Dana Ross, B.Sc., is gratefully and proudly acknowledged; she did an excellent job teaching her father a physics lesson.

BIBLIOGRAPHY

1. Halliday, D. and Resnick, R., Fundamentals of physics, New York: John Wiley and Sons, Inc., 1970.

2. Hecht, E., Physics in Perspective. Reading, Mass.: Addison-Wesley Publishing Co., 1980.

3. Keating, J., "The Two Faces of Sport," Proceedings, The First Canadian Symposium, The Philosophy of Sport and Physical Activity, P.J. Galasso, Editor, Sport Canada Directorate, Department of Health and Welfare, Ottawa, Canada, 1972, pp. 103-118.

4. Simon, R.L., Sport and Social Values. Englewood Cliffs, New Jersey: Prentice-Hall, Inc., 1985.

5. Thomas, C.E., Sport in a Philosophic Context. Philadelphia: Lea and Febiger, 1983.

6. Young, H.D., Fundamentals of Waves, Optics and Modern Physics. New York: McGraw Hill, Inc., 1980.

LIST OF CONTRIBUTORS

The Rev. Richard C. Adams is Associate Professor of Philosophy at Quinnipiac College, Hamden, Connecticut, where he teaches philosophy and comparative religions. He conducts courses in the philosophy of sport, and is a member of the Philosophic Society for the Study of Sport and of the Sport Literature Association. He is also a member of the Temple of Understanding, a non-profit educational corporation which sponsors programs which are concerned to promote understanding between the religions of mankind, and unity and peace in the world.

Frans De Wachter is Professor of Philosophy at the Catholic University of Leuven (Belgium). He teaches ethics, ancient philosophy, and philosophy of physical education. He has published articles in these three domains. He is a member of the Executive Committee of the Philosophic Society for the Study of Sport.

Sean Egan is a Celt from Ireland. He teaches at the University of Ottawa. An avid sport enthusiast, he boxed nationally and internationally for ten years. Presently, he swims and runs the odd marathon. He speaks Gaelic and French fluently and loves Gaelic music. He was educated in Dublin and Paris universities. He has a Ph.D. from the University of Oregon.

Michele Gelfman is head women's tennis coach at the University of Notre Dame, Notre Dame, Indiana. The 32-year old Brooklyn, New York, native received her B.S.E. degree from Northeast Missouri State University in 1976 and Masters in P.E. from Indiana University in 1977. She coached successfully at Beloit College, Valparaiso University, and Western Illinois University before becoming the head Irish coach in 1985. She has compiled a ten-year coaching record of 234-82. The Notre Dame women's tennis program has been elevated to the NCAA Division I level.

Ms. Gelfman's professional playing accomplishments include competing on the Penn circuit. She is an active member of the United States Professional Tennis Association and the Intercollegiate Tennis Coaches Association as well as the United States Tennis Association. She was the Indiana State Director of Tennis for the Special Olympics in 1986 and is again in 1987, as well as being the Director for the International Games being staged at the University of Notre Dame in the summer of 1987.

Edward W. "Moose" Krause retired in 1982 as Athletic Director from the University of Notre Dame. For over 45 years he has been deeply involved in Notre Dame football and athletics, from his days as student recruit and player under the legendary Knute Rockne, through his time as First Assistant and Head Line coach under Frank Leahy, Head Basketball coach, and into his tenure as Athletic Director through and beyond the era of Ara Parseghian. He is a two-time All American in football, a three-time All American in Basketball, and a member of the Basketball Hall of Fame. He played professional basketball for the Boston Goodwins and the New York Celtics for eight years from 1934 to 1942. He also played and coached with the Lithuanian National Team for the 1936 Olympics in Munich.

Mr. Krause was assisted in recording his reflections by his son, The Rev. Edward C. Krause, Ph.D., who is an Assistant Professor of Liberal Studies at Gannon University in Erie, Pennsylvania. After graduating from Notre Dame, Father Krause did advanced work at the Gregorian University in Rome, Italy, and completed doctoral studies at Boston University in Massachusetts. He taught at Stonehill College, North Eaton, Massachusetts, and at St. Mary's College, Notre Dame, Indiana, before going to Gannon.

John W. Molloy, Jr. has been the Sports Information Director at Brandeis University, a Division III school with 21 intercollegiate teams, since August 1985. Prior to that, he spent nearly two years as Sports Information Director at Quinnipiac College in Hamden, Connecticut. While at Quinnipiac, he had responsibilities for 11 intercollegiate sports. John Molloy has worked as director of media relations for the Pawtucket Red Sox, the Triple AAA International League baseball team. His previous experience also includes internships in the sports information offices at Dartmouth College and the University of Pennsylvania. Mr. Molloy, a native of Quincy, Massachusetts, was graduated from Boston College High School in 1978. He is a 1982 graduate of Saint Anselm College with a Bachelor of Arts degree in English. He is a member of the Philosophic Society for the Study of Sport, of the Sport Literature Association, and of the College Sports Information Directors of America.

Linda Morgan, mother of three athletic daughters, holds a B.A. degree in Sociology from Kansas Newman College. She played varsity basketball in high school and continues recreational basketball in her leisure time. Linda is currently vice-president of an academic publishing house.

Saul Ross, Ed.D., is an Associate Professor in the Department of Physical Education, School of Human Kinetics, University of Ottawa. His area of specialty is the philosophy of physical education and sport, with particular interest in epistemology, theory of action and theory of persons. His experience includes ten years as a secondary school physical educator who also coached thirty teams in five different sports. He is a theoretical practitioner and practical theoretician as well as a life-long athlete who continues to play racquetball, as a sport, for recreational, athletic, and health purposes.

Albert K. Wimmer, Ph.D., currently teaches German language and literature at the University of Notre Dame. He has two sons, both of whom were involved in collegiate sports; Steve played tennis, and Marc is currently a senior at the University of Southern California with a swimming scholarship. Dr. Wimmer taught tennis for many years to toddlers and young adults.

INDEX

Dallas Cowboys, 80
Davin, M., 43
da Sena, Fernando, 11
Detroit Red Wings, 5, 78, 82
Dorais, Gus, 64

Eastern Massachusetts Super Bowl Title, Division II, 83

Faust, Gerry, 69
Festinger, L., 24, 30
Fianna Eireann, 37
Fighting Irish, 8, 43, 44, 45, 64
Fionn Mac Cool, 37
"Four Horsemen," 67, 68

Gaelic Athletic Association (G.A.A.), 36, 40, 41, 42, 43, 44
Gaelic Athletic Games, 36
Gaelic Football, 40, 41, 43, 44
Gaelic Games (Modern), 40, 44
Gaelic League, Women's Division (National Language Movement), 40
Gardiner, E. Norman, 5, 14
Gibson, Althea, 3
Gipp, George (The "Gipper"), 63

Halloran, J.D., 25, 30
Hartford Whalers, 79
Hecht, E., 111, 113
Heinilä, K., 28, 30
Heisman Trophy, 68
Helsinki Conference 1975, 1982, 17
Hesburgh, Father Theodore M., 65, 74
Higgs, Robert J., 4, 12, 14
Highland Games of Scotland, 36, 38, 39, 40
Highland Gatherings, 38, 39
Huizinga, Johan, 2, 3, 6

Orwell, George, 21
Ottawa, University of, 45
O'Tuathaigh, G., 42, 48
Owens, Jesse, 26

Parseghian, Ara, 63, 64, 65
Pax Olympica, 27
Plato, 2, 3, 12
Prince of Wales, 39
Pro Bowl, 85, 86
Puirseal, P., 43, 49
Pulford, Bob, 80

Racquetball
    doubles, 103, 105, 106
    as athletics, 107, 108, 110
    as play, 109, 110
Redmond, G., 40, 49
Rice, Grantland, 6
Rockne, Knute, 63, 64, 65, 66, 67, 68, 70, 71
Rourke, Jimmy, 84
Russell, G.W., 22, 30
Ruth, Mike, 85

Saint Paul, 72
Schmidt, H.D., 24
Seattle Seahawks, 5, 84, 85, 86, 87
Sherif, C.W., 22, 23, 31
Shriver, Eunice Kennedy, 54
Simon, R.L., 108, 113
Sinden, Harry, 79
Sigliago, Joe, 68
Sipes, R., 22, 31
Smerlas, Fred, 84
Socrates, 3
Sorin, Father Edward. C.S.C., 10
Special Olympics, 6, 53, 54, 55, 56
    First International 54, 56, 57
    First International Winter, 55
    International 55, 57